GEORGE BARKER

Twayne's English Authors Series

Sylvia E. Bowman, *Editor*

INDIANA UNIVERSITY

George Barker

 90

George Barker

By MARTHA FODASKI

Brooklyn College

Twayne Publishers, Inc. :: New York

to the man who dreamt of sea turtles

and to Steven, Corinna and David
who were chased into the sea.

Acknowledgments

For the American rights to all of his poetry except *The True Confession of George Barker,* I am indebted to George Barker. For permission to quote from the latter I acknowledge The New American Library. A portion of this book was published by Trident Press in 1966 in *Master Poems of the English Language,* edited by the late Oscar Williams. Oscar Williams enthusiastically supported the project, as he did the poet; he believed in both. I am indebted to the Southern Fellowships Fund for two grants which enabled me to finish the work, to Paul Wiley, Gian Orsini and the late John Enck of the University of Wisconsin who read an earlier version of the manuscript. Sylvia E. Bowman offered helpful editorial suggestions. I am especially grateful to my mother Allie and my late father Ralph Haller (the man who dreamt of sea turtles), without whose supererogation as grandparents the expense of spirit would have been too great. Finally, I wish to thank Kevin Sullivan of Columbia University who took time from his busy schedule to read the manuscript with his usual editorial and critical acumen.

Acknowledgments

Preface

GEORGE BARKER (1913–) is an established modern poet who has not been given sufficient or wholly accurate critical attention. This study aims to make reparation for the neglect, as well as to explain it. Based primarily on Barker's poems, it explicates, evaluates, and locates the poetry in its proper historical and literary context, one that is in almost every detail Romantic.

After an introduction to Barker's expressive, dialectical poetic theory, which derives from the English Romantic tradition, the opening chapter examines his view of the poet's function and his relation to twentieth-century offshoots of Romanticism—the New Apocalypse and Surrealism. The book then moves through the poetry in chronological order, stressing illustrative poems, to emphasize the range and line of Barker's development. Barker's novels and plays are treated only when they illuminate the poetry.

In reviewing the early work, the second chapter indicates the early *leitmotifs*, such as the pursuit of vision and the preoccupation with sex; Barker's inability to ignore the Auden group reveals, however, his political and literary awareness. Chapter Three analyzes his major work on the growth of the poet, *Calamiterror*, which traces the artist's development from egoism to another center—one disclosed in Chapter Four to be the poet's social responsibility in a world at war. Chapter Five focuses on the *Sacred and Secular Elegies*, a work that embodies the concept of the tragedy of modern man's spiritual predicament; it examines the love poetry, lyrical expressions of the symphonic dilemmas of the Elegies. Chapter Six reveals the poetry of the 1950's to be a series of studies of Byronic man haunted by guilt and doubt, torn between pessimism and need for affirmation. The seventh chapter deals with later verse, which reflects the comforts of friendship, the solaces of places, the inspirations of travel (cf., for example, "Flight 462," *Poetry*, CX (April, 1967), 38)—or infects the reader with barbs of irreverent satire.

Barker's work always manifests Romantic faith in the individual. But the rival claims of scientific determinism and transcendental vision inevitably create a poetry of conflict, which polarizes the pull of the instinctive life and religious feeling. The poems themselves become affirmations that transcend subject matter full of antinomies. Barker has always sought music and imagery to assert and reconcile his contrary emotions. The young poet-*voyant* of the mid-1930's uses words primarily for their evocative power; the poet-prophet of the 1940's uses them expansively as tokens for things, events, and people that serve as part of a symbolic or metaphoric commentary on the modern world; the poet-Dionysus of later poetry writes of personal struggle for tragic affirmation.

The final chapter discusses Barker's controversial reputation. It asserts that critical response, which is largely confined to the cursory consideration of book reviews, often reflects the biases of "New Criticism." Reviewers too often suspected Barker's expansive verse and the proliferation of his poems—and, despite the approval of "New Romantics," his work was too often dismissed without serious study. But analysis need not clip the wings of Barker's butterflies. Although he occasionally descends to the bathetic or the banal, his best work is remarkable, a richly musical, emotionally compelling poetry of fearless moral vision, recording one modern man's struggle with darkness and hope for light.

MARTHA FODASKI

Brooklyn College

Contents

Chronology

1913   George Granville Barker born February 26 in Loughton, Essex of English father George and Irish mother Marion Frances Taaffe. When six months old, moved to Chelsea in London where his father was a constable. They were, according to *The True Confession of George Barker,* "a little low/In the social register."

1927   Left Regent Street Polytechnic, a secondary school to which he had transferred from Marlborough Road Elementary School. Worked at numerous jobs such as wallpaper designer and garage mechanic.

1932   Reviewed *New Signatures* for *The Adelphi.*

1933   *Thirty Preliminary Poems* and *Alanna Autumnal,* his first novel, published. Met T. S. Eliot.

1935   *Janus,* second novel, published. *Poems* published by Faber and Faber. Married Jessica Woodward. Left London to live in a Dorset cottage. Received grants for further work from Faber and Faber, the Royal Society of Literature, and the King's Bounty.

1937   *Calamiterror* published.

1939   *Elegy on Spain* published. Went to Japan as visiting professor of English literature at the Imperial Tohoku University in Sendai.

1940   *Lament and Triumph* published. Came to United States, stayed with Oscar Williams and his wife Gene Derwood, remained in the U.S. until 1943, living in both New York and California.

1941   *Selected Poems,* first American publication, appeared. Wrote a series of book reviews for *Nation* and prose and poetry for *New Republic.* For Oscar Williams' *New Poems: 1940* he wrote a foreword; his poetry occupied thirty pages of the anthology.

1942   Recorded poems for the Harvard Library.

1943   *Sacred and Secular Elegies* published by New Directions as number five of "Poets of the Year" series.

1944   *Eros in Dogma* published. Returned to England. Lived in London until 1945; then in Essex, 1945–1948; then in Haslemere, Surrey, in 1949.

1947   *Love Poems* published in New York.

1950   *News of the World, The True Confession of George Barker* (Part I), and *The Dead Seagull*, a novel, published. Began a series of travels. Despite his wanderlust, he has always been involved in domestic relationships: his poetry reveals his affection for his mother, his artist brother Kit, his sister, and his nine children. Spent 1950 in Italy.

1951   Spent in Spain where he was made an honorary bullfighter. Between 1951 and 1956 he divided his time between London and Barcelona.

1954   *A Vision of Beasts and Gods* published and made a selection of the British Poetry Book Society.

1957   *Collected Poems* published. Came to United States, lived in New York City. Traveled to the western states and spent some time in Las Vegas.

1958   *Two Plays: The Seraphina* and *In the Shade of the Old Apple Tree*, verse dramas originally written for the BBC, published. Read his poetry eloquently but reservedly at the Poetry Center of the Y.M.H.A. in New York City in November. On December 15, he read and recorded poetry at the Library of Congress.

1959   In spring read poetry at thirteen American colleges and universities over a period of thirteen weeks. Then returned to England.

1960   Went to Italy. Remained there until summer of 1963 when he divided his time between London and Rome.

1962   *The View from a Blind Eye* published. *Penguin Modern Poets* 3 (Barker, Martin Bell and Charles Causley) published.

1964   *The True Confession of George Barker* (I & II) published in New York. Traveled between Italy and England. "Memorial Stanzas for Louis MacNeice" appeared in *Poetry Magazine*, April 1964. "Formal Elegy on the Death of Oscar Williams" appeared in *Poetry*, February 1965.

1968   Still itinerant, Barker currently makes his home base 9 Quick Street, London N.1.

CHAPTER 1

Barker's Esthetic: Dynamic Philosophy

G EORGE BARKER'S poetry discloses a fundamentally Romantic and religious sensibility. Keenly aware of the magic and mystery of language and of the trial and tragedy of human life, his first-person speaker is seer and sinner, apostate and aspiring saint. Questor, prophet, interrogator, supplicant, or critic, he struggles to resolve contradictions between feeling and thought, gratification and guilt, and the beast and god in man. His early (1933–1937) and middle (1938–1949) poetry batters at the dark mysteries of idealism, sexuality, war, and man's spiritual isolation. His later poetry (1950–) is often chastened, sometimes spare and lyrical, sometimes direct and satiric in its impatience with the demons in the modern world or in the human breast. For Barker, poetry is spiritual autobiography.

One of the rare modern poets wholly dedicated to his vocation as poet, Barker wanted, as he himself wrote of André Gide,[1] to write his life and have it too. He also wanted to read it. His literary excursions started early. The essay "Coming to London" outlines the most important—"certain books and the eccentric consequences of reading them."[2] Reading Byron at the age of nine inspired him to design his own tomb. Reading Spenser inspired his first poem, a "monstrosity" called "The Tournament." He left school at the age of fourteen, but his eclectic education went on. At fifteen, he was impressed with the experimental frankness of James Joyce's *Work in Progress;* but he marked the end of his childhood with his profound reaction to first reading T. S. Eliot's "Ash Wednesday."

In 1931, equipped with little formal learning but with fierce determination to be a poet, Barker met John Middleton Murry, who introduced him to Michael Roberts, editor of *New Signatures,* the anthology that was to be instrumental in announcing the new poetic voices of the decade. Upon its publication in 1932,

15

Murry asked Barker to review *New Signatures*, as well as F. R. Leavis' seminal study of modern poetry, *New Bearings in English Poetry*. The review in *The Adelphi* applauded the new poets, who Barker (like most literary cognoscenti) thought were shrugging off the Eliot influence; he was more impressed by William Empson's ambiguity than by W. H. Auden's social poems.

Impressed with the young man's review, Michael Roberts sent Barker to David Archer's bookshop where he met David Gascoyne, the avowed Surrealist poet, and Geoffrey Grigson, editor of *New Verse*, who was preparing the first issue of his magazine. By the time his first poems were published in 1933, Barker had read the major modern British writers, including Auden, Spender, and Day Lewis—the Pylon group. Shortly thereafter, the young autodidact was probably reading Dylan Thomas, for Thomas' "When Once the Twilight Locks no Longer" and "I see the Boys of Summer" appeared in the June, 1934, issue of *New Verse* and "If I were tickled by the rub of love" was printed in August. Barker himself was to be a contributor in October of the same year. Although Barker tried to strike out in a new direction, he did not develop in a literary vacuum.

The publication of his first novel, *Alanna Autumnal* (1933), made the impoverished young writer no money; but it did gain him "the friendship of Edwin Muir." After David Archer printed *Thirty Preliminary Poems* (1933), Barker showed Muir a "harder poem" about his adolescent searchings; Muir sent him to T. S. Eliot at the *Criterion*. "And that was how my Poems [1935] came to be published." [3] Faber and Faber continued throughout the years to be Barker's principal publisher. Despite several attempts to differentiate himself from the older poet whom he called "tame Apollyon," [4] Barker continued to consider Eliot his mentor.

Where Eliot was calm, Barker was audacious. Besides what Barker gained from literary contacts, perhaps the most important influence on his early life was his militant declaration of the poet's right to experience. It had disillusioning, almost disastrous results. In 1932, his "imagination militant after mystery," [5] Barker blinded his brother Kit in the right eye in a fencing match. No doubt it was an accident, but in his "Funeral Eulogy for Garcia Lorca," [6] the young poet tries to justify the act as part of the development of a poet, who is a rare and prized human being. But thereafter the Romantic anarchist with a conforming conscience felt that he bore the mark of Cain.[7] By 1933 he had "informally" resigned from the Catholic church.[8] After his marriage in 1935 he became the itinerant poet-pariah whose life was the history of his travels and his loves, and whose poems recorded his sense of alienation. A sojourn in Japan was followed in 1940 by a trip to the United States where he informally ended his marriage. Despite frequent returns to his native England and periodic residence in London, he was, thereafter, the artist in exile, pursued by personal furies. His wanderings took him chiefly to Spain; to the United States, where he was seldom happy; and to Italy, where he found a measure of solace. Perhaps his chief solace was writing poems.

I *A Romantic Esthetic*

Barker is a poet, not a theorist. He wrote only one brief article[9] and a foreword for an anthology[10] which deal specifically with the poetic process. Nearly every review he wrote indicates, however, his deep concern with the poet's method and mission. His early novels *Alanna Autumnal* and *Janus* touch upon the poet's problems. Three essays ostensibly about other matters—"Poet as Pariah," "William Shakespeare and the Horse with Wings," and "The Face Behind the Poem" (an essay honoring Tennyson)[11]—really justify his approach. The poems themselves sometimes deal with and, of course, always exemplify his attitudes. Many concern the poet's role. But, characteristically, Barker has never formulated a detailed, systematic program.

In lauding Shakespeare, Barker writes: "This passion for baring all things down to the nerve and the bone . . . is what, in the end distinguishes the greatest of poets. . . . The great intelligence at work on fundamental explorations of the human spirit operates in a more intuitive manner than the mundane mind. This manner is, I believe, a poetic operation. . . . Its truths are perceptive and poetic. And, like poems, they do not offer themselves up to the examination of the scientific or rational judgment." [12]

Distrustful of science and rigid rationalism, Barker contrasts intuitive and conceptual knowledge and insists that the former is poetic. He cannot accept Eliot's self-consciously reasoned esthetic. He dislikes the strain of dogmatism and deliberate intellectuality he finds in William Empson, Maud Bodkin, and I. A. Richards, whom he calls Cambridge Positivists.[13] He opposes the "intellectual self-consciousness that paralyzes the poem even before it is written." [14] Elsewhere he writes that "the act of poetry must be performed in a sphere removed from the function of judgment if it is to succeed as an act of poetry." [15]

Barker also believes in originality. The fictional young man in *Alanna Autumnal* says "I shall (if I can) in poetry describe my fanatical belief in unique startling singularity." Sensing that he isn't being original, he continues, "If I have imitated any author it has been surreptitiously done by the hand which springs in my belly and works from there" (31). The author, writing in the stream-of-consciousness, was probably imitating Joyce and Hopkins who loved "All things counter, original, spare, strange," and to whom Barker later acknowledged his indebtedness in a sonnet. Barker's passionate desire for individuality parallels Hopkins' theory of individuation.

Such idiosyncratic poetry is inspired by the need for esthetic purgation. In the 1934 *New Verse* inquiry, Barker announced himself "sceptical of Freud," but he could not ignore him. While Barker's sexual symbology, his agonies over sexual necessity, and his explorations of dream psychology attest to the Freudian influence, his remarks on artistic sublimation suggest it. Like D. H. Lawrence, he finds fault with Freud at the same time that he affirms the importance of Freudian subject matter. *The True Confession of George Barker (I)* notes cynically that "The sulking and son loving muse/Grabbed me when I was nine. She saw/It was a question of self abuse/Or verses . . ." (15).

From the start, Barker felt that the poet cooks in the witch's brew of his feeling and that his suffering, more intense than that of other men, inspires and produces poems. With typical energy, passion, and defiance, he announced this esthetic in "Therefore All Poems are Elegies," the foreword to Oscar Williams' anthology *New Poems: 1940* in which Barker relates poetry to powerful feeling. Byron considered poetry to be the expression of excited, volcanic passion; Keats' criterion of excellence in art was intensity; and Barker's expressive theory of the poet's darkly magnificent epiphany places him in the Romantic tradition:

That moment of truth when God with the sword in his hand profiles in front of the poet to deal him the kill of a poem is the moment when the poet sees home to the heart of things: the inspiration which is an assassination. . . . To be so closely caught up in the teeth of things that they kill you . . . is, truly, to be a poet. . . . It is around the fundamental and impossible mystery of existence that the poet wraps his paroxysms; because he is the captive of his senses. . . . The skill in living for the poet is, as for the lover, to reach a paroxysm most often but at least expense of spirit. For this reason the prospect of political accident cutting short the life appears as ridiculously irrelevant. I am in the grip of a struggle which is far more terrible and far less noisy. . . . Against this Demagorgon [the force of death] the poet is Perseus who cannot win, but captures a head each time a poem is written. Therefore all poems are elegies and the real grief is the possibility of joy.

The poet-hero, dramatically confronted with his inspiration, is filled with a double sense of power and weakness. He becomes a Perseus battling the monster death, because the poem is a commitment to life. He is compelled to create a poetry of conflict out of the struggle between Eros and Thanatos, the creative drive and the death wish.

When the young man in *Alanna Autumnal* wants inspiration, he cries like an idealistic Longinus with the voice of Joyce's Leopold Bloom, "Sweet God, into me secrete the amazing juice" (5). The image, glandular, almost sexual, is an appeal to the irrational divine afflatus. In *Calamiterror* the speaker invokes the west wind, emulating Shelley, to render him Yeats' kind of eternal artistry— "the nightingale's bough" (25). Even the jaded speaker of *The True Confession of George Barker* appeals to the muse of inspiration with "send/The spell that makes the poem live" (22). In 1953, using Pegasus as his symbol, Barker defended inspiration in a lecture commemorating Shakespeare's birth; poles apart from the analytical critic who prefers poetry with a core of discursive logic, Barker writes that poetry is essentially mysterious and is under the "absolute power of the poetic imagination." [16]

When Barker writes of "those antithesis [*sic*] in whose proper interplay the work of art ideally consists. See Coleridge on the Dialectics of Verse," [17] he picks his ancestry, an esthetic of the imagination which Coleridge called "dynamic philosophy." Barker's dramatic need to reconcile opposites is reflected in his interpretation of Keats' negative capability: the "supreme neutrality that appears to deprive the poet of his personal character and make of him a creature half subhuman and half superhuman. . . . The opposite and antithesis of the withdrawal from life achieved by the religious mystic. . . . The poet is a man who has elected to love all things, even all unlovable things, because he cannot exist in the abstract; he is bound to and by all objects and subjects." [18] The negative capability, for Barker, only *appears* to mean loss of personal identity; like his artistic sublimation, it has little to do with the process of depersonalization; it is not an escape from personality or withdrawal from life. Barker, a spokesman for dynamic philosophy, cannot ally himself with Eliot's cult of impersonality.

In calling the poet half subhuman, half superhuman, Barker reveals his special concern with dualities. Spirit and flesh, emotion and belief are opposites to be synthesized by the interplay of the creative faculty and, as Barker puts it, the material, ephemeral world. He writes that the "imagination and the mundane cross" in the "no man's land" which, it seems, is the "spiritual state" or "intellectual condition" of the artist. His "spiritual state is passive and negative; his intellectual condition is neutral, and his emotional atmosphere is chaos. The relation of these conditions is dialectical." [19] Although passivity and supreme neutrality are not ordinarily associated with a Barker poem, the dialectic accounts for the warring polarities and paradoxical nature of much of the poetry. When the artist's emotions tell him of human suffering and his intellect of the absurdity of effort to stop it, the tension produces "the angle of the detached and tragic . . . which is the condition in which the chameleon prevails." [20] In calling the poet "a chameleon," Barker acknowledges his debt to Keats with whom he would agree that "What shocks the virtuous philosopher delights the chameleon poet."

Early poetry treated the "unspeakable categories," such as hermaphroditism, narcissism, the death wish, and the birth trauma. Investigating human behavior, especially the poet's own, was both his duty and his privilege. He turned to Shakespeare as his authority for the "rigorous luxury of being able to put anything—anything at all—into a poem." [21] The poems stem not from a determination, therefore, to affront the squeamish reader but from Barker's initial belief in the poet's responsibility. Ultimately, the pull of biological necessity and poetic privilege against a Catholic sense of guilt (he had resigned from but not relinquished his religion) creates a poetry of conflict.

Nevertheless, in 1954 Barker reiterated Archibald MacLeish's axiom that a poem should not *mean* but *be:* "Poems do not have to do anything at all or be anything at all except operating poetry. They need not persuade us of the immortality or the mortality of the human soul, or cure the stammer, or provide an alternative to the act of religious worship: all they have to do . . . is to convince us that at the moment of reading, nothing else matters." [22] Elsewhere Barker alleges that Eliot confused art with religious ritual and that Matthew Arnold confused it with morality.[23] Such pronouncements are more assertions of romantic self-sufficiency (and, ironically, of awareness of current critical attitudes) than truth about Barker's own subject. A far cry from *poesie pure* is his idea that poetry explores the human spirit by seeing "home into the pattern of . . . individual existence." [24] The "writing of a poem comes very near to telling . . . a colossal lie" and yet its aim is "the pursuit of truth." [25] The "lie" of metaphor discloses higher truth. And the poet conveys that truth as "the enemy of society," a pariah, an indirect critic and unacknowledged legislator of the world.[26]

Consonant with the pariah's serious purpose is his desire to create memorable speech. He depends on auditory and rhetorical effects. In 1934 Barker disaffiliated himself from Imagism and objective reporting; in the *New Verse* inquiry he asserted that his stimulus for writing was verbal rather than visual. The late poetry sometimes relies on accurate description when reporting an actual event, but the interest in language per se that spoiled some early poems becomes, later, the wit, paradox, and punning that contribute surface interest to irreverent, satirical poetry. As his talent matured, Barker refined his style so that he could create brilliant imagery and magnificent musical effects that were often a perfect reflection of his stormy romanticism.

II *The Poet's Role*

Barker repeatedly examines the poet's role. In three stages parallel to the lines of his development, he changes from idealist to realist to tragic yea-sayer, although the poems are often ambivalent. The poet is first seer, then, responding to the Spanish Civil War and World War II, prophet and gadfly of the state, and, in the poetry after 1950, Dionysian artist—sometimes the tormented questioner, sometimes the guilt-ridden tragedian, sometimes the antichrist, sometimes the ironist directing barbs at himself and whoever displeases him, and sometimes the saintly cynic.

For the *New Verse* inquiry Barker, at the age of twenty-one, defined poetry as spiritual unraveling. The speaker of the early poems burns "to be easy air." "Daedalus" (1935) sets up the antitheses of trancendental yearnings and the awful fact that they are doomed to drown in physical reality. Like Rimbaud's *voyant,* the young poet seeks the unknown. In *Janus* he writes that "My purpose, then, may be thus summarized: I repeat to that worn eye, *the sky is there* and *there is the sky.* And to those myriad of eyes which, being unworn, immediately discern the sky, I say, remove the eye and thus become the sky" (92).

In 1950 Barker described his youthful preoccupation with spiritual vision as parallel to Stephen Dedalus' epiphany in James Joyce's *A Portrait of the Artist as a Young Man.* Barker invokes his early ecstasy in language reminiscent of Stephen's first experience of mortal beauty:

> Come, sulking woman, bare as water,
>   Dazzle me now as you dazzled me
> When, blinded by your nudity,
>   I saw the sex of the intellect,
> The idea of the beautiful.
>   (True Confession, I, 22)

That Barker at first thought of his speaker as a poet-mystic is clear in *Calamiterror* (1937) which records, however, the realization that mystical withdrawal and identity with the absolute are impossible: the world is the poet's proper subject. A key poem in relation to Barker's development, *Calamiterror* is a twentieth-century *Endymion* in which the lesson of human sympathy must be learned—or a modern *Prelude* in which is revealed the growth of the poet's mind from self-love through love of the world to love of his fellow men. In *Calamiterror* the poet-*voyant* becomes, therefore, the poet-*engagée.*

Barker had in his first poems felt the Leftist influence of the Auden group; in 1935 he wrote "The Bloom of Creed." Geoffrey Grigson, in whose *New Verse* Barker published, admittedly preferred poetry with a political purpose. In the late 1930's Barker contributed to *The Left Review,* among whose contributors were Auden, Spender, Day Lewis, and Hugh MacDiarmid; and in *The True Confession* (I) Barker admits that he once "entertained the Marxian whore" (31). His 1938 "Note on the Dialectics of Poetry" expressed a new concept of the poet's function; the poet has "a specifically acute instinct about human desires and aspirations . . . he must acknowledge the obligations upon him of stating these desires and requirements. . . . The poet is the voice of the servile by which their need is heard." [27]

The world situation made expedient "a purely temporary practical attitude which, as against the fundamental 'spiritual' attitude, we may term the immediate or 'political' attitude," because only thus could the poet hope to "render tolerable both his immediate circumstances and the circumstance of his inherent insignificance. . . ." [28] Poems such as the *Elegy on Spain* (1939) and "Vision of England '38" were written from such a stance; without being actually hortatory, they envision a terrifying world situation and pray for or prophesy delivery. Barker espoused "the negative propaganda to be achieved by illustrating merely the processes of decline inherent to capitalist society. . . ." [29] Actually this is the approach the Pylon poets used most of the time, but Barker's poetry is distinguished by its passionate involvement. Like his contemporaries, however, Barker felt that the "poet militant" had as much chance as the politician to cure the world's ills.

The prophet usually begins with evidence of the world's sickness. Soon after *Calamiterror* Barker wrote "Resolution of Dependence" which signals the poetic stance of much of the middle poetry (1938–1950). In it Wordsworth says "I see/That already your private rebellion has been quelled./Where are the violent gestures of the individualist?" The poet resolves to "fix on the facts," to have faith in the "interdependence of the parts." Thereafter Barker was, in theory at least, to insist that the poet is involved in mankind. A comment on Blake, Barker's symbol for the visionary, reveals the new attitude: "When the poet aspiring to the superior love of the mystic, divests himself of his devotion to all created things, then you get the Prophetic Books of William Blake. They are magnificent, but they are not poetry. For a metaphysical poem—if the word is used exactly—is a contradiction in terms. Poems are as thoroughly caught up in physical things as a junk merchant." [30] But, he writes, elsewhere, that "It is, surely, possible to put too much responsibility upon the facts in a poem." [31]

After the middle period when the poetry reflects his response to world crisis—after World War II recedes into history—Baker espouses the idea, announced in his 1953 Shakespeare lecture, that "poetry is at bottom acceptance of life" (420). He might have found echoes of his idea of tragic affirmation in the philosophy of Eric Gill or in the poetry of Dylan Thomas or of Yeats, to all of whom he dedicated poems. The idea probably derives, however, from Nietzsche (whom Barker calls a "Dionysian") whose Dionysus suffers, not from the impoverishment Barker sees in Eliot but from overabundance of life. Dionysian art is, like love, an intoxicating, ecstatic, whole-hearted commitment. In the *New Verse* inquiry Barker remarked the association of art and love when he said his attitude toward poetry was amorous; in "Therefore all Poems are Elegies" he associated poetic and erotic paroxysm. The seeds of his yea-saying were sown when he wrote that tragic resignation "supplies the poet with that absolute negative on which the positive of life can gloriously or ingloriously inscribe itself." [32] Nietzsche's theory of self overcoming, like Blake's annihilation of Selfhood and Yeats' projection into the mask, suggests the dialectic that produces the transcendental affirmation of dynamic philosophy. In 1954 in "Letter to a Young Poet," Barker clarified his role:

> I speak of the whispering gallery
> Of all Dionysian poetry
> Within whose precincts I have heard
> An apotheosis of the word
> As down those echoing corridors
> The Logos rode on a white horse;
> Till every No that sense could express
> Turned to a transcendental Yes.

III   *Barker and Apocalypse*

Poets of the New Apocalypse found in Barker their unavowed prophet. In the 1941 anthology *The White Horseman,* writers like Henry Treece, J. F. Hendry, and G. S. Fraser advocated the return of freedom for the artist. They said that man should have "greater freedom, economic no less than aesthetic, from machines and mechanistic thinking"; that the individual is all important; and that myth is "a personal means of reintegrating the personality." [33] They opposed to a mechanistic an organic view of life and advocated organic form in art. In *How I See Apocalypse* Henry Treece included a chapter on the tree as a symbol for unity; Barker's 1935 poem "The Cornucopia" anticipated Treece's view and his symbol. E. F. F. Hill, a less restrained exponent of the Apocalypse, wrote: "The disclosure of horrors is not an entire vision. . . . The symbols matter little before the passion of the spirit which breaks into song. The horror *and* the song, the great Whore *and* the Bride, evil *and* good, death *and* life polarized, in rhythmic wholeness. . . ." [34] The impassioned concern for polarities, as well as the desire to inform all experience through imaginative vision, is exemplified in Barker's work.

The emphasis on man's freedom, hence on his responsibility to make choices, leads to the concern with human conduct notable in Barker's poetry and, for example, in poetry of David Gascoyne, Alex Comfort, and a poet of religious feeling like Anne Ridler, all of whom are related to the Romanticism of the 1940's. Furthermore, the eschatological world view, suggested even in the name of the group, finds ample precedent in Barker's middle poems which indeed assume that we live in the imminence of doom. To themes of time, death, loneliness, and love are "added the themes of emotion and feeling accentuated and accelerated by the crisis-psychology of war." [35] The Apocalyptics could have derived their program from Barker's verse.

The Apocalyptic Personalism advocated by Stefan Schimansky suggests Barker: ". . . the Romantic must discover, out of suffering and despair, his own style and approach, must because of his divine spirit display his individual vision, that hallmark of the unique personality." [36] The integration or release of personality, like man's freedom, ". . . can only come to him from within, for he alone can discover his vocation and be its final judge; no one else, no individual, no collective group can take away this duty and fight his personal battles in his personal world. This is the mainspring of Herbert Read's concept of Anarchism." [37] A thorough-going modern Romantic seeks a personal system by which to come to terms with the world. Vigorous assertion of his individual rights is revealed in his attitude toward subject matter and language. New Romanticism accepts anarchic experiment as well as

quiet lyricism, because both tacitly exemplify its first principle—
that art is above all self-expression; that personality, the sense of
involvement, and emotional communication are primary.

To substantiate such theory the 1940's poets looked back to the
Elizabethan rather than the metaphysical tradition. Barker's ear-
liest tastes were for Thomas Campion (and Shelley), and Shakespeare was his bulwark. In *How I See Apocalypse*, Treece says
that Shakespeare is the new poet's model, and that the modern
movement derives primarily from an English background which
includes Webster, Blake, and Revelations[38] (presumably the King
James Version). At the same time the new Romantics were not
afraid to turn to nineteenth-century writers like Tennyson (as
Barker did in "The Face Behind the Poem"); one member of the
group, John Heath-Stubbs, wrote a study of Thomas Lovell Bed-
does. Barker, even more obviously a Romantic than the group that
tried to appropriate him, often goes directly to the Romantic
poets.

According to Frederick Hoffman, the Apocalypse derives in
part from D. H. Lawrence, although the new poets were in no
strict sense his followers. They shared his distrust of mechaniza-
tion and modern society. Like him, they substituted a mythological for a clinical approach to the unconscious.[39] Although Apocalyptic theory asserted the value of using, like the Surrealists, the
materials of the subconscious and the dream, it was positive
"where Surrealism had been negative." [40] Freud and Jung, as well
as Lawrence and mythmakers like Joyce, form a background for
Apocalyptic thought. The new program "in a sense derives from
Surrealism, and one might even call it a dialectical development
of it; the next stage forward. It embodies what is positive in Surrealism. It denies what is negative—Surrealism's own denial of
man's right to exercise conscious control. . . ." [41]

It is not surprising to find the work of the avowed British Surrealist David Gascoyne represented in Romantic anthologies, nor
is it surprising to discover that in 1941, in notes on contributors,
Poetry Magazine called Barker a "Surrealist."

IV   *Barker and Surrealism*

Most of Barker's early and middle work appears to deny self-
conscious control. Certain early poems, such as "Narcissus III,"
"The Amazons," and "Daedalus" seem to explore the unconscious

through psychic automatism; but Barker is not merely a passive catalyst (as, indeed, avowed Surrealists rarely were in practice). "The Amazons" exhibits, for example, a serious concern for deliberate structure. But the setting in the unconscious, the hallucinatory dream atmosphere, the subject matter of the liberated unconscious suggest Surrealism. Wallace Fowlie has noted that the Surrealist reenacts the myth of Daedalus as an exercise in the will to free himself from objects surrounding him;[42] Barker's "Daedalus" is just such an exercise.

Barker's concept of poet as mystic or transcendentalist probably owes more to his preference for Blake, Shelley, and Yeats than to his awareness of Rimbaud or Surrealism, despite his acquaintance with David Gascoyne. He would, however, assert with the Surrealists "that by spiritual means they would achieve the liberation of the human mind." [43] He is, like them, barraged by the influence of Marxism which prompted English apologists to assert that Surrealism is basically materialistic and would not distinguish between mind and matter. Barker never fails to make the distinction; and, even as his tragic view deepened, he preferred being called an incomplete transcendentalist to being called a materialist.[44] He could not wholly accept the materialism which underlies Surrealism and its benefactor Freudianism.

His dialectical esthetic echoes, however, the Surrealist approach to art. Herbert Read writes that the artistic process corresponds to dialectical materialism; there is "a continual state of opposition and interaction between the world of objective fact—the sensational and social world of active and economic existence—and the world of subjective fantasy." [45] Read's statement in *Surrealism* (published in 1936 by Barker's publisher Faber and Faber) anticipates Barker's "Note on the Dialectics of Verse," except in the fact that Barker's English seriousness and Irish passion find no room for the word "fantasy" or for the fantastic humor which attaches itself to Surrealism.

Like Dylan Thomas' dialectic, Barker's has an aura of high seriousness. Thomas, calling his method "dialectal [*sic*]," described a process like Barker's except for one vital difference: Barker's thesis is the poet's state of mind, his antithesis the world situation; whereas Thomas centers on "the motivating center, the womb of war."[46] Despite his interest in words *qua* words, Barker places considerable emphasis on content. But, like Thomas, he sees art as the interplay of antitheses, the product of a dialectic in process with no resolution except in and through the art form.

V   Two Souls in One Breast

Barker chooses his tradition. The Romantic ideas and attitudes in his poetry are modified by his personality, by his sensitivity to the social and intellectual scene, and by a dynamic of conflict which arises between the claims of Catholicism and his anarchic Romantic sensibility, or between the claims of naturalism and vision. The conscience plagues the natural man; the realist tempers transcendent yearnings. Hoxie Fairchild's definition of Romanticism might well describe Barker's poetic mission: "Romanticism is the endeavor, in the face of growing factual obstacles, to achieve, to retain, or to justify that illusioned view of the universe and of human life which is produced by an imaginative fusion of the familiar and the strange, the known and the unknown, the real and the ideal, the finite and the infinite, the material and the spiritual, the natural and the supernatural." [47]

Fixity and rigidity of belief are polar to Romanticism which focuses on pursuit and is, by its very nature, with the being who is its center—the Romantic artist—constantly changing. In his personal religion everything is bifurcated, but he seeks a way to transcend contradictions. Despite the self-disgust of the natural man, he inscribes joy upon life through the creative act. Despite the ugly and base, he discovers wonder and mystery through tragic acceptance. Barker's need to unite the beast and god in man is expressed in his late definition of the poet as "a mystic who operates downward. He operates downward upon the world through the agency of the word, perceiving that every object enshrining a divine idea, is therefore to be loved. And such love does not need the dogma of the Church: it only needs victims." [48] Barker's explanation suggests his subject, his distrust of dogma, and his approach through concrete experience—through the object upon which the predatory imagination goes to work. Most of all, it reveals his psychology.

The Romantic psychology, not to say theory, is full of antinomies. When Barker refers to love and victims in the same breath, he reveals a basic ambivalence. The classicist would object to this perpetual dualism:

The classic objection to romantic psychology is that it accepts an inner dualism—two souls in one breast. . . . In romanticism the two souls can be variously interpreted. I have chosen as most basic man's double consciousness of power and weakness. Another way is to take it as the Christian conscience faced with good and evil. A third way is to view it as a conflict between man's sense of values and his knowledge that nature is indifferent, which is another form of Pascal's loneliness in the eternal, silent spaces.[49]

Jacques Barzun's definition distinguishes the Romantic from other forms of the modern ego, which accept direction from external sources such as society or institutionalized religion. Barker persists in his inner dualism, alternately despising and marveling at his own feelings. He is both an instinctive earthbound Cain and a visionary Able. As Cain, he is repeatedly drawn to sensational subject matter; for the violent natural man, the center of conflict is sex and his special connection of sex with sin. As Abel, he seeks to affirm man's spirit and his God. Barker integrates or transcends the polarities in the dynamic philosophy of his poems.

CHAPTER 2

Early Poems: The Desire of the Moth

ALTHOUGH *Thirty Preliminary Poems* (1933) is, as the title suggests, tentative and exploratory, it contains the seeds of the subject matter and style that Barker was to develop. Fundamentally subjective, idealistic, and suspicious of materialistic values, the poems deal with the conflict between the claims of self-knowledge and social awareness. Many announce the importance of the individual's sensations, feelings, and ideals; others reflect the dominant concern of the 1930's with social change. The young poet seems to be trying to decide whether to follow in subject matter and technique the example of his contemporaries or to strike out in the direction of his inclinations.

I Explorations

The incipient poet-*voyant* exhorts "Chalk-chasing children" to follow their easily erasable souls. ("Each man's soul is his chalk.") From the start he feels impelled to explore all aspects of life—the realm of Being ("the stars") and of Becoming ("the oceans")—and to suffer all the agonies, to know "all worst throes." Already we see the outlines for the conflict between transcendental escapism and the pull of experience. In "The Immeasurable Expanses of Despair," Barker denies the world of Becoming with "nowhere/ Lies entirely about us," and nearly denies Being too with "Being I see studded with mirages/Lures us poor hopers along endless mazes." He concludes, however, that the most courageous course is to travel "along the rainbow's line"—to seek the mysterious unknown.

A typical poem, "Ode to a Dead Aeronaut," combines the modern image of the pilot, like the airmen of Spender and Auden, with the traditional implications of Icarus' flight. Barker's flier is a somewhat anachronistic modern idealist whose soaring imagination suffers eclipse. Although the developmental pattern is hazy, the poem is clearly based on the contrast between the idealist, probably a Shelleyan poet who travels "The excursionistic/Coast of the imagination," and the crass materialists who "lie awaiting/ The fall of the soaring soul." The *persona* looks nostalgically to a past in which the feats of transcendent imagination received their due: "All prosperous soil was once/A volatile body which on bright wings/Within the mind's bright winds sped/Skirting the barren expanses, over the earth." In the modern era imagination is put to use in selling products such as the "vegetable oils" advertised on the billboard into which the airman crashes. The attempt to live the life of mind and spirit ends in ignominious and ironic descent through "profane edifices," the signs which are the only things the ineffectual angel destroys in the enemy's camp.

"No Feeble Dream . . ." reveals Barker's affinities to the activism of the 1930's. In expressing distrust of the dream so important to Symbolism and Surrealism, it can be read as an oversimplified response to the Apollonian and Dionysian modes of existence: "Saps away courage the dream/Like semen, breeding nought but fear. . . ." Even the sexual reference typifies the 1933 poems. Also characteristic is the Audenesque inversion: "Their fever to act than dream/Desires aspirations is more worth." The license for the colloquial "keep on the move" comes from the 1930's poets. But Barker mixes liberated language with abstract, latinate words such as "pellucid," "deviation," "aspiration," and "illusion." Like the other poems, "No Feeble Dream" is almost free of allusions; a single biblical reference to Bethlehem is typical. Writing in free verse, Barker experiments with internal rhyme, revealing an obsessive interest in words and sound per se that sometimes obscures, but never really leads him away from, ideas.

Some of the irregular sonnets deal with ideas and attitudes current in the 1930's. By juxtaposing the historical crucifixion with a modern form of punishment ("Crisscross of cables this wicker electric chair/He sits, staring at the telephone like a cross"), the first sonnet somewhat obscurely reminds us of modern man's self-martyring complacency and his failure to sympathize with Christ's radicalism. The plea for action, presented in techniques reminiscent of Eliot as well as of Auden, is similar to the Pylon group's answer to Eliot's mood of interrogation: "(Father, why hast Thou forsaken us?)/We cannot interrogate, there is not time/Immediate work's to be done, and done by us." Sonnet 6, like Yeats' "The

Second Coming," suggests that the end of the Christian era is near; it attacks the "impotent Jesus," implying that His martyrdom led the way to "the final ebb of decay" in the Western world.

Barker's flirtation with Marxism is also evident in these early poems. Sonnet 8, like Spender's "The Express," connotes motion into new eras: "Like trains, like the wind, go forward, like the tempest/Precipitates its power, we eliminate chance. . . ." The poem dismisses the world of *The Waste Land* as "The aridity that is past" and naïvely asserts a future that "shall come round on the globe again and reap/The gift of our rain with gifts of bloom." The journey motif, the breaking from the past, that underlies Auden poems such as "To throw away the key and walk away" (*Poems*, 1928) and "Chorus from a Play" (which appeared in *New Signatures*) is evident in Sonnet 9 where "We nakedly address our tryst-like journey/To cities whose startling buildings rest/Fairly between earth and air. . . ." "We Cannot Parallel" looks forward to a time when hunger and old values will be discarded. The line "They may/Loosen loves rule and sometimes travel nude" strikes out against conventional bourgeois love. But, true to Barker's latent pessimism, the poem ends with:

> May not in progressive pace the wonder of the race
> Quicken, an evening sun, but one
> Remembers in contemplating the sun that as the sun
> Disappears, our despair may equal their despair.

Although many of the poems suggest the influence of the Auden group, others concern the adolescent's discovery of his body and of the close connection between erotic pleasure and pain. Sonnet 4 contrasts parts of the body to objects from the outside world (and anticipates the startling imagery of later poetry): lips which are "worms" incongruously placed on "your concrete barred reinforced body . . . /Are wrong for you, like a plum in a mountain/ A plum of contagious pudendal emanation." Another poem explores with disgust and fascination the adolescent's vulgar approach to sex: "feeding the mind with quick/Monosyllabic maxims, our hot body arms." "Love Poem," a prelude to later love lyrics, indicates that "Love's stroke lamed" him and "set/In radiant circle/My imagination/Racing." Love is a "withering ecstasy."

Perhaps the most interesting erotic poem is "Poem on a Dream" whose subject is self-love and the search for identity. In *Poems* (1935) it is called "Narcissus I." The speaker relates a dream in which he received an unforgettable kiss from an unknown person. In reality he searched everywhere for his lover and finally discovered him in a modern equivalent of Narcissus' pond—the windshield of his car. Although the poem is not in itself a remarkable achievement, its candor is.

Barker has, however, renounced all except two of these first poems; for only "Narcissus I" and "Verses for a Nursery Wall" are included in the so-called *Collected Poems* (1957). "Verses for a Nursery Wall" is an anomaly in the first volume, for it attempts to convey anxiety objectively, entirely in terms of a distorted symbolic narrative. The direct, detached, economical Audenesque nursery rhyme language and singsong rhyme are in direct contrast to the other poems:

> The cat and the mouse
> Fear the rat and fear
> The man with the hat
> And the house and spear.

The poem reveals perhaps better than any of the others the influence of Auden.

At the same time that these early poems reflect contemporary influences, they reveal interest in poetic tradition. The choice of genre titles—the ode, the elegy, the eclogue, the sonnet—is at least tacit admission of the search for form and discipline which has been Barker's persistent task. But the "Ode to a Dead Aeronaut" is less an ode than an elegy. The "Elegiac Stanzas" do not so much lament death as, in the spirit of Barker's early nihilism, they look forward to "Erasure of our pain." The eclogues seem to get their titles from their natural imagery. Rhyme and meter in the sonnets are irregular; often Barker approximates the traditional octave and sestet with breaks at the end of line nine or ten. In reality the preliminary poems reveal little genuine concern for metrical discipline or formal organization, despite their attention to sound and words in themselves. What they do indicate is a predisposition toward a lyrical, self-centered poetry and a preoccupation with the dominant intellectual mood of the decade.

II   *Spectres and Stars*

Almost all of *Poems* (1935) might be called "spiritual unravel-ing" [1] in which the poet searches for an idiom and style appropriate for romantic subject matter—subjects such as death and muta-bility, the search for self-knowledge and self-identity, the explora-tion of love and frustrated idealism. A notable achievement, "The Amazons," represents the exotic blossoming of Barker's symbol of death as oppressively female. "Dark Dreadful Death" in *Thirty Preliminary Poems* suggested death to be a *femme fatale*. The nausea of the young nihilist in Barker's 1935 novel *Janus* ends in a death wish concerning "no skeleton death, but an atemporal and aspatial female" (17). "The Amazons" invokes the *femmes fatales* of death, frightening, but fascinating, repulsive but compelling. The poem's atmosphere and dislocated imagery are Surrealistic. The mind is the seat of the drama. The language—intricate, per-sonal, and emotive—turns away from objective reality to the dream and unconscious reality. The appeal to violence that char-acterizes Surrealism is incipient in the controlling Amazon image —"They are the ambush. . . ."

The phantasmagorical setting is a landscape including clearly defined objects in unorthodox combinations defying the logic of reality—a landscape like that of a Dali painting. In it fantastic creatures, like those in Chagall's painting, literally flow about. The phantoms move in "the palaces/Appearing brilliant on the moun-tain tops" among the "lemon trees . . . colonnade[s] . . . [in the] glade" of the "land Unbeing," a vacant place like the setting of a Chirico painting. This land is "within the dark places/Of the heart," where the "Queen Masters," like Circe, "compel/Like up-right beasts men into that shambles/Death's press of doom and blood." The death wish, like the sexual urge, is compulsive.

Carefully chosen adjectives reveal the tone of the poem and nature of the spectres—"pale," "phantasmal," "pallid," "miasmal," "hypnotic," "ominous." Barker uses the present or past participle ("appearing," "rehearsing," "whispering," "haunting," "hanging," "hewn," "flown," "blasted," etc.) in preference to action verbs, to create the feeling of movement and yet of suspension in a dream world where normal syntax and natural time and cause-effect rela-tionships are missing. Verbs, such as "moan," "sway," "presses," "strike," "compel," are, however, carefully chosen to convey mood.

Inverted syntax retards movement, helps communicate the hallucinatory vision, and heightens the anxiety.

The poet creates a unity of sound and sense. The music of "The Amazons" reproduces the dreamlike atmosphere and the opulent movement of the irresistible giantesses. Liquids and nasals used alliteratively and internally create the quiet, insistent flow. Sibilant music and onomatopoetic effects make for a remarkable correlation of sound and sense. Despite the success of its evocative mesmerism, Barker in effect renounced "The Amazons" when he omitted it from the *Collected Poems*. It represents much that the poet came to distrust—dream, passivity, nihilism. Nevertheless, it is perhaps Barker's best, among the many poems he wrote at this time, about death.

The "Elegy Anticipating Death" deals with the theme in a symbolic framework borrowed largely from Dante. In a modified terza rima with basic images of "abysmal catacombs" and "branches of flame," the poem uses figures of the hallucinatory vision as extensions of an internalized, personal hell; psychological search is given a physical setting. "The Tenements of Death" also attempts to define death symbolically. The tenements, crowded homes of the disinherited dead, are themselves personified as ghostly spectres, located somehow in a cosmic setting and simultaneously in the bed of a dead man. The poem asks us to visualize, superimpose, and identify utterly unrelated images. Instead of emphasizing and communicating feeling, the montage technique is confusing. The central symbol does not adequately control the poem; the images are paradoxical and centrifugal. Nonetheless, the "fiery grating" and "heatless lave of dark river," which at first glance seem carelessly brought together as images of death, can perhaps be justified, like the whole poem, as suggestive of the paradoxical and uncertain nature of death. Such a Surrealistic poem is the antithesis of the almost anachronistic "Luctus in Morte Infantis," notable for its Platonic idealism and its affirmation of the life of the soul. Generally similar to Milton's "On the Death of a Fair Infant," Barker's poem is informed by the mythopoeic idea of starry lights representing innocent souls returned to clouds of glory.

Although death inspired the young writer, the moment of fulfillment in life also intrigued him. A short lyric, "The Crystal," which Yeats included in *The Oxford Book of Modern Verse*

(1935), celebrates the value of the gem-like moment reminiscent of Walter Pater's precious flame:

> With burning fervour
> I am forever
> Turning in my hand
> The crystal, this moment.

Such ardent hedonism is an augury of Dionysian yea-saying. "Paradisiacal Bird" is even more specifically a glorification of the urge to live; the bird "Of plumage flame" is the "Life-phoenix" with "wings of love" who is exhorted to

> Flame with all glory
> . . . against
> The awful dark falling
> Time of death.

In "The Seal Boy," the speaker, apparently watching a seal in the surf, achieves a time spot, a moment of great joy. The seal "diving under/The great tidals" is transformed into the "moving ecstatic boy" responsible for the instant of bliss, "Sliding through the gloomy seas" to "bring me pearls." The beauty of the animal's movement is captured by the beholder; the seal boy harbors in the speaker's "wild grip" as he apprehends the moment of vision when the creature becomes a symbol of fulfillment—the rare pearl, the kiss, the ecstasy.

Perhaps the major subject of *Poems* is the "vision-chaser." "The Wraith Friend," another poem Yeats selected for *The Oxford Book of Modern Verse*, begins almost like Eliot's *The Lovesong of J. Alfred Prufrock*—"Following forbidden streets/Towards unreal retreats" in search of consolation for "my burning miseries/ Miming the stars." The speaker supplicates the wraith spirit, the Icarus of man's aspiration who "climbs/Eagerly to heights of the skies" although "known flesh must fall/Soon within this prison's wider wall. . . ."

Barker's major record of frustrated idealism is, however, "Daedalus." Clearly influenced in conception and technique by Joyce, the poem explores the implications of escape from the labyrinth of sensual life by heroic flight. The speaker is Daedalus contemplating the remains of the fallen figure of his son (although Icarus' name is never used, for Barker wants to imply that Daedalus is looking at his *doppelganger*.) The death of the hero, "Formed in fearlessness," who like Blake's Orc dared to challenge heaven, stirs the *persona* to thoughts of his own approaching demise, which will be dishonorable. Past heroism is ironically contrasted to modern ignominy.

The difficulty of "Daedalus" is immediately evident:

> Like the enormous liner of his limbs
>   and fell.
>   Remain behind, look on
> What's left of what was once in blighted remains.
> That imponderable body
>   Smote my desire, now smitten
> Mortally.
>   I lift his head, his death dampens
> The moist palm of my hand like handled fear
> Like fear cramping my hand
>   and stand.
>   Remain behind, entertain posthumous fear.
> I entertained.

"His" death creates fear, who thus becomes another character in the poem—the "Spectre" whom the speaker addresses in Part II as he entertains his own painful uneasiness.

The Spectre is ironically an essential part of inner reality. Daedalus invites the ghostly fear into the world of the subconscious:

> Come where no crowds can trouble us divert us
> No acrobats no hawkers bottles or street musicians
> No towering necks like buildings overlook
> Intimate revelation.

The concrete visual effect suggests painting; the acrobats tempt one to think of Picasso's *Les Saltimbanques* which informs Rilke's *Duino Elegy* V in which the acrobats symbolize human activity. Barker's symbolism is similar, but his canvas is more crowded. Away from the carnival signs of the absurd reality of the modern world, the speaker leads Fear into the world of memory, "Across morning haunted lawns in earlier/Days," to show him the Daedalus of the past, the talented, heroic maker (like the archetypal poet) who once dared a great flight. This Daedalus had once been a whole man who was haunted by no Blakean Spectre, unknown to Fear. Now, contemplating his own youth, he remembers his identification with the defiant Icarus who dared to seek the sun. While fearless, Daedalus' double did not fall, but "recently sure has fallen from that high/Platform." However, in his fall the vision chaser at least "evaded" the Spectre.

Daedalus is, as Part III reveals, prohibited from following the fallen spirit; but existence is intolerable without him: "We cannot be/While he is gone from being." Daedalus realizes that the fallen figure is really his alter ego, his spirit, the opposite of his present fear. The Spectre of self-dividing fear who spreads "Internal dissension" has cut Daedalus off from his courage, leaving him "Sick with his not being" and "Empty with his going." Having died in heroic defiance of human limitations, Icarus has arrived at the doom to which Daedalus must go: "Where wander those once known herons/Or rabbits . . . killing have known" (IV).

The final section of "Daedalus" (V) compares the descent of Icarus to that of the more cautious protagonist, a modern man related to J. Alfred Prufrock. The heroic fall, like that of Satan or Prometheus, "in the combat/With forms invisible intactual" is contrasted to the speaker's degrading descent. Daedalus' modern counterpart drowns in the "Lethal water" of Becoming.

Logical (or chronological) progression is distorted by the speaker's complex anxieties. Conventional syntax often breaks down; subject or predicate, in the intensity of experience, gives way to fragmented utterance. The elliptical distortions reveal the effects of spectral fear. Obviously, such a poem cannot be read with the usual apparatus of poetic apprehension any more than *Ulysses* can be read as a conventional novel. Given the central symbols of the archetypal idealist and the disillusioned maker, the other symbols fall into an associational pattern revolving around the contrast between the free spirit of the past and the earthbound modern creator who is cut off by fear from the heroic life of the imagination.

The presence of the Spectre in "Daedalus" suggests that Barker had been reading Blake's prophecies and, in all likelihood, Middleton Murry's study of Blake;[2] for Murry had acted the role of mentor for the young poet some time before *Poems* was published. In the chapter "Los and the Spectre" Murry identifies the Spectre as Urizen (reason), the lord of this world, who is opposed to Orc, the energetic, passionate son of Los, who is variously interpreted as a personification of poetic genius, creativity, or the prophetic imagination. Like Daedalus, the maker, Los is the blacksmith creator with a fiery son. Murry says that Orc (like Icarus) represents the righteous rebellion of the instincts against "False Reason"—against Urizen's sole domination.[3] When Barker's hero was a unified personality, he had the Identity of which Middleton Murry speaks and which Los, the poetic imagination in Blake, labors to reëstablish. In a sense, then, "Daedalus" deals with the issues of Blake's Prophecies or at least with those issues as Murry interpreted them. Barker's poem goes beyond hypostatizing aspects of a single personality; it might be said to deal with the traditional and modern Romantic. Blake's Orc and Shelley's Prometheus defy the infinite; Barker's hero sadly recognizes his descent to the mundane.

"I am that Face about which Fire Fell" is perhaps about the same Icarus-spirit or even about the figure of Los which Blake illustrated and called a "terrible flaming Sun"; Blake's engraving of his vision of Los pictures him in a globe of flame.[4] Barker's visionary identifies himself with light, with the sun, with the "soul" striving "for its flight." Barker combines concern for such idealistic search with the theme of mutability in "Have Travelled that Vernal Avenue," whose central image, a spatial conception of the temporal theme, is the avenue of youth. The speaker is at first troubled over letting youth slip away without having made any important choices. He achieved no important goal, was granted no revelation: "Nor does that avenue turn over mountain,/Intersecting dark like lightning heavens. . . ." The avenue turned "towards easy heavens,/Down valleys, through cities, turning to the off-fountain/Of love, ejecting a waterless yearning."

Although the geographical landscape for a psychological journey is reminiscent of Auden, Barker's poem has no political overtones. The young man, suspicious of "the pale ghoul of Youth," pursues it, only to find that it is himself. The search for identity results, paradoxically, in the desire to escape from self; but the quest ends with the admission that "I am my hateful lure/Like lust in mirrors." The final stanza is a rhetorical question such as Milton and Keats had asked themselves: "Must I thus, vision chaser, my major time betray?" It questions wasting "the great preparing/Of soul, bright sign, as victorious ray/To fix upon the mountain top of Love."

In "Have Travelled that Vernal Avenue," as in "Daedalus" and "The Wraith Friend," Barker uses internal monologue to present the divided self. Such a schizoid quality underlies the three Narcissus poems, all of which deal with aspects of the second self and with the search for integration and individual identity. Like "Narcissus I," "Narcissus II" treats the effort to find love. The setting of the earlier poem is restricted to the area of social activity; but "Narcissus II" ranges through "The forest of the universe,/And heaven's uneasy fields." The psychological journey to revelation is given a cosmic geography. Wandering through "chaotic hills" is the "brown Narcissus," the shadow, the "vagrant self." But the speaker assures his alter ego, "I penetrate the valleys bringing correct direction:/Love's compass is the self,/And never, half by half,/Could vagrant self detect correct direction." Instead of the brotherly love, which means correct direction to Auden, Barker's speaker first needs proper self-love. When the speaker and his *doppelganger* are unified, the man gains his identity.

The best Narcissus poem, "Narcissus III," is less objective than the first and less concerned with identity than the second. As a vivid hallucinatory dream based on the tension between the horror and fascination of self-love, it is more intensely realized than either. The masochism underlying narcissism is suggested when the persona asks the Narcissus of his dream to

> Render me with love insensible—
> Still I will seek your lips and seek
> Your overpowering to overpower
> Our deformed amour to conform in sleep.

He envisions coitus with this shade of himself:

> Triple lipped Apollo, I consign
> Your visitation to the night,
> When, amid cavernous mislove, your orbs,
> Large with anticipate lust must diminish
> As, beneath my smothering embrace,
> The shocks your nine limbs striving to impart
> Shudder into the gentle heaving of sleeping.

Perhaps Barker is thinking of Nietzsche's Apollo who represents the art world of dream, the opposite and necessary partner of Dionysus, union with whom produces tragedy. The ecstasy is surely the Dionysian rapture of pain and pleasure.

Apollo, being "tripple lipped," suggests the hermaphroditic nature of the dream. The triple lips may also be genitalia, and one of the nine limbs, the phallus during the fantasized union. Fearful anticipation and morbid fascination culminate when the dreamer dismisses the "abhorrent presence," appalled by the "ardour" of their meeting "As with passionate fear I clasped your animal head/And hid my knees in the flowers of your bowels." The lust is animal; the decadent eroticism, horrifyingly convincing. Although the poem is a successful example of the young poet's explorations of "unspeakable categories," an older Barker did not include it in the *Collected Poems*.

The 1935 volume contains conventional love poetry too. "Lax though the longing may wear" is an irregular sonnet idealizing immortal beauty. "I am the Land, Surrounding Sea" asserts the dependence of the beloved upon the lover and, at the same time, their interdependence. Based on a Donne-like correspondence and less ambiguous than Dylan Thomas' "Where once the waters of your face," this Barker poem deals with the same comparison. "The Land is You," another love sonnet, develops the correspondence between the earth and "us." "The Poppy Trembling" says that love is the creator of beauty in nature. In "His Perennial," the creative principle is, however, supremely neutral. The ceaseless work of Love's hands reveals "His indifference"; the disinterested divine Eros forces "A stricter vitality/Into the reservoir/Of our behavior." In the canon of Barker's work, "His Perennial" is the first of a long line of poems treating the indifferent but perpetually creative element which is, paradoxically, basically ruthless, destructive, and perennial to threaten lovers with the responsibility of offspring.

A more sensuous and consistent poem about creation is "The Cornucopia," a poetic description of germination and the fruits of creation, in which vegetable is compared to human growth. The horn of plenty described is the poet-*voyant*'s ideal man, an organic whole whose abundance is his selflessness, a "mature tree" who can face the elements and the parasites and yet represent a spiritual haven. The comparison between the growing man and the plant gathers at the conclusion to the definite image of the tree, the strong selfless, Christ-like figure, the mystic for whom souls are the true reality. Poems such as "The Cornucopia," "The Constellation," and "The Chimera" are charged with enthusiastic idealism.

But, although the bulk of *Poems* traces the desire of the moth for the star, at least three poems—like some of his earlier poems— indicate Barker's social awareness. "The Leaping Laughers," "The Bloom of Creed," and "Northumberland, Bound Down" are politically motivated. "The Leaping Laughers" seems at first militantly Communistic:

> When will men again
> Lift irresistible fists
> Not bend from ends
> But each man lift men
> Nearer again.

Because the poem looks simultaneously toward the biblical past and toward future heroism, it cannot, however, be called Marxist. The image of leaping and the challenge of "tall walls" reflect the energetic idealism of the whole volume. It is Blake crying for Orc, or Nietzsche crying for a superman; its activism reflects a desire to believe in the perfectibility of man. It asks for courageous action, although "the fallen stoop over stones."

With a studied disregard for anything like the vocabulary of social realism, a second political poem, "The Bloom of Creed," treats the growth of a militant, yet spiritualized, political ideology "born across the racks of want/And of despair." Having arrived at a "pacific" state of resignation, the "eye" can accept violent means toward a just end—it "Halts at no murder-turning," for the "Quick ill biting" of revolutionary action makes "winds/Of new summer ease everywhere." In "Northumberland, Bound Down," an occasional poem of social protest, Barker personifies Northumberland in her economic distress. He denounces the "beast [that] to the breast clamours" for taking "from her bowels . . . the black streams" of coal from Newcastle, "So cheated, so deceived" by the ungrateful capitalistic beast of Southern England. The poem reflects the social unrest of the decade in which starving men from Northumberland made hunger marches on the south of England.

The distinguishing theme of *Poems* is the unabashed search for a vision of the Ideal. The central tension arises, however, from the discrepancy between the real and the ideal. The internal journey motif and theme of frustrated quest mark the poems. Barker's reinterpretation of myth in terms of twentieth-century consciousness points in itself to the influence of Eliot and Joyce; the symbolic hypostatizations indicate the influence of Blake. In order to display divisions of internal reality, Barker envisions the constituents as separate entities, just as Blake did in a larger setting. Unlike Blake, Barker sets aspects of reality at large in the individual consciousness. Psychological actualism is basic to the technique of the most successful poems.

The vocabulary reveals something of the struggle within the dual personality. Barker repeatedly uses verbs such as "search," "wander," "leap," "spring," "rise," and "fly"; in the key poem "Daedalus" such words are juxtaposed to verbs like "fall" and "descend." Things representing the soaring spirit and the infinite are used obsessively—birds, spirit, soul, stars, cloud, sky, wind, heavens, angel, and sun. Fire and light imagery repeatedly suggests ardor for the ideal. Juxtaposed to symbols for the infinite are objects standing for the flux the *voyant* wishes to escape—the seas, oceans, river, earth, land, world, flowers, and imagery of the body. Natural and anatomical imagery celebrates love and the fever for action. "Love" as an absolute, as a symbol for creativity, and as an emotional value is, with "time" and "death," basic to the vocabulary.

Except for the sexual imagery, the language is not peculiarly modern. In fact, the latinisms, archaisms, and poeticisms of the *Preliminary Poems* are still sometimes present. "Daedalus" with its poetic "Hark," its latinate participles "visitant" and "preparant," and its generally dignified vocabulary illustrates some of the strengths and weaknesses of style. In poems of idealistic aspiration, images sometimes become nebulous and distorted, as the moth seems to fly in wild abandon at the star, to make a quick thrust at the unknown and then to fly at it from another angle, desiring to become "One among the wild stars wildest. . . ." Often the young poet is carried away by the hypnotic power of sound; his orchestrations sometimes lack subtlety. Interest in sound leads to a strong reliance on alliteration and repetitions, such as "where once he trod/I cannot tread," "forced/To force from her source," and "calls/And recalls the call." This leads to tautologies such as "Like mourners the stars mourn their light." At its worst, the style is needlessly wordy; at its best, it puts wordiness to work to evoke mood.

With *Poems* Barker emerges as an individual poet whose interests look back to the Romantic period and, in part, to French Symbolism[5] and forward to the New Apocalypse. He is, however, constantly aware of the current developments in English poetry. His Romantic sensibility is tempered by twentieth-century awareness. A motto which suggests both the attitude toward language and the central theme might be Shelley's:

> The desire of the moth for the star,
> Of the night for the morrow,
> The devotion to something afar
> From the sphere of our sorrow . . .

CHAPTER 3

Calamiterror: *The Mind of Man My Haunt*

IN 1953 Barker wrote that the truly great poet fearlessly enters the "ontological cave of origins." [1] In *Calamiterror* (1937) this is literally what he did. The poem might be considered an example of the Jungian archetype of transformation; but the archetype is the Romantic poet, who, in searching the mind of man, detaches himself from the ego to find another center. *Calamiterror* is Barker's magnum opus about the conflict between the poet-*voyant* and the poet-*engagée*. In it Barker turns from a concept of poet as seer to listen to the still, sad music of humanity.

I *The Reintegration of Personality*

Jung's *The Psychology of the Unconscious* deals with the "song of the moth" which indeed typifies Barker's *Poems* (1935). In the chapter on the "longing for the Beyond," Jung asks the question which is the key to *Calamiterror*: "What is to be the way out between the Scylla of renunciation of the world and the Charybdis of the acceptance of the world?" [2] Barker attempts to find the answer by "going into the darkness, to . . . a meeting with the Shadow, actually the inner realities of a man's own unconscious." [3] The Romantic poet, interpreting Jung almost literally, plunges into himself to search for integration.

Calamiterror is, then, a poem of quest; it is also a poem about the individual's apprehension of the calamity of modern life—personal, social, and cosmic. Although the portmanteau title conveys the central mood of fear of disaster, the conclusion of the poem asserts that there may be escape from the cycles of anxiety in a kind of dialectic of freedom. This dialectic is, in fact, Marxist, specifically related to the Spanish Revolution. The poem moves from the disaster of subjective reality to the world of fact, equally painful except for the hope for a synthesis. The development is in one sense from a search for a personal religion to the discovery of

a political ideology. The quest for the Father of the universe in
the early sections is essentially the same that occupied Joyce; like
the religious seeker, the speaker would lose himself to find himself; like Blake, he is preoccupied with the annihilation of Selfhood. Barker's theme is the reintegration of personality.

II *The Traumas of Selfhood*

The dedication preceding the "Introductory Stanzas" and ten
books of *Calamiterror* actually introduces the dialectic of the
poem, for it compares Albert Gordon Barker to Abel and Barker
himself to Cain, an *enfant terrible* whose psychological growth
the poem traces. Specifically, it is an apology from the guilty
brother who had put out Albert Barker's eye. In the spirit of Jew-
ish law, the Cain of the story offers the poem as recompense for
his deed: "I render to my Hell hand's Abel/The no less agonized
blood my hand has bled." Cain and Abel are the dualities of the
poem. Where Cain dominates, the visionary Abel is lost; when the
Self is cast off, the dualities are integrated. But Cain's world inspires the calamiterror.

The mood and setting are established in "Introductory Stanzas
to Book I." Modern life is comparable to Plato's cave, Wordsworth's "shades of the Prison house," Rilke's City of Pain, Eliot's
Unreal City:

> The gay paraders of the esplanade,
> The diamond harlequins, the acrobats,
> The gloriously lost in summer glades,
> The wanderers through the acropolis,
> The ones who seek the times' shade
> Reclining by castastrophes,
> The figures of the downward grade:
> The gay shadows of the shade.
>
> The continental operas, the play
> Featuring beautiful beasts and the beast beauty,
> The shimmering mannequins of Love's display
> Meandering through, glamorous and nude,
> Loose at the hip; those whom they displease,
> The glancers at the gay boy's beauty;
> The mirror-gazer self-betrayed;
> Loving shadows in the shade.

Jung writes that the shadow is the collective archetype which "can in large measure be inferred from the contents of the personal unconscious."[4] Barker immediately sees the whole of modern society as representing this dark side of life. The constituents of the shade are legion. Its occupants, who seek empty diversions, are gay carnival figures or tourists who watch but do not participate in life. Their interests are sophisticated, empty, and sensual. Love in the shade, as in *The Waste Land*, is hollow and unreal—for "shimmering mannequins"—or perverse, homosexual or narcissistic. The "geography of shade" is nature made unnatural: "The falling cliff . . . leaves a stare"; "cataracts . . . grave/The private gardens." The National Trust and Kensington Avenue are the scenic spots in an empty, materialistic society.

The "fourth dimension/Of this space" is fear (Stanza 4), which is all pervasive, part of the past, present, and future as we grow away from original innocence: "The three figures that forever stand/Beside, before, behind; as we grow older/Achieving mass as we become the shade." Turning from the dimensions of the modern horror, the speaker asks whether there is an escape for the spirit; and he concludes that, in a life of preoccupation with Self, there is none: "The one always remaining in/Self's skin, remains a shade." In Blake's terms, Selfhood must be annihilated; in Jung's terms, the ego must be transformed if the personality is to be integrated. The cave of modern life suddenly shifts to the microcosm, the "abdominal abysms" of the individual unconscious, the womb world of the infantile personality. The self that must be transcended is a "mask" (Stanza 6), completely external, superficial, sensual, provocative, yet vacant and empty—a "half-filled mask" like the men of Rilke's *Fourth Duino Elegy*. Barker writes:

> The mask of self though more than marvellous,
> Glancing through ovals lovelier than Hylas' eyes,
> Speaking with the tongues of the girls on the isles,
> Languishing lips, coloured and loose
> Like fruit, suspended and melodious:
> The countenance of vacancy,
> The cardboard opera facade,
> The empty stare that does not see,
> The speech of shade.

After questioning the nature of the face behind the mask of man's physical existence, "Introductory Stanzas" concludes by interpreting the face, enforcing a basically dualistic concept and suggesting that the divine is present in every man; the divine becomes man, a microcosm where he is both creator and created, where he has ironically become the self-centered individual of the shade. Blake believed in the god-man, and Jung has recently written that *"Christ exemplifies the archetype of self,* a son of God *sine macula peccati,* unspotted by sin."* [5] Christ, who had won against his shade, Satan, watches those for whom he suffered and, it seems, is called back to suffer again because man is still in the realm of darkness. But Barker means more than this, for he is preparing for Book I in which the archetype of innocence is born, trailing clouds of glory.

Book I gives us the birth of the babe into a chaotic world of flux; even at birth, the division in his nature is clear:

> What when born upward breaking from heaven downward
> It is my bare bloodred babe, with beauty
> Branching from armpit, maypole at thigh, world flying
> Like fairboats around, the axis of existence.
> The bud beginning, the burning salamander
> Suspended in his breast, the shambles in the bowels,
> The tall tree spine supporting vertical
> The crucified to life bare body blood.

For Barker, as for Jung (and Heraclitus), the pattern of reality is "a dynamic system in which a central energy perpetuates itself by opposing forces which, though apparently antitheses, are found to be phases of one cyclical process." [6] The antitheses here are spirit and flesh; the god of "Introductory Stanzas" is forced into life. The babe "with beauty/Branching from armpit" is related to the creator-made-flesh from whose arms tendrils "break out." The images of the Heraclitean flux, of breaking upward and falling downward, reveal the combination of mundane and celestial elements. The babe (and the phallic "maypole") is the "axis of existence," the microcosm, center of the egocentric world. Barker's dualistic infant possesses a soul ("the burning salamander") and fallen flesh ("the shambles in the bowels").

Life as the newborn sees it is the subject of Stanza 2, which juxtaposes macrocosm and microcosm to develop the tree comparison. Subject and object are willfully mixed: leaf and eye are joined for the infant who explores the world of sensation. The eye and leaf are the same thing, both aspects of the microcosm, interchangeable since the babe is a tree, an extension of nature. "The eye-shaped leaf" examines heaven; "The leaf-shaped eye examines/The eye-shaped leaf," and "each observes in each/Heaven and heaven." The babe is narcissistic. His admiration is self-generated, although the heaven he sees may be the glory from whence he came.

Unfortunately, the abandoned and the dead also go to the shade of life. Everything is cyclical. Images for a horror movie call up the distasteful mating which perpetuates the life cycle:

> It is here the hooded vulture and the walking
> skeleton
> Converse in fatal language, rend each other,
> blend together.
> Here on the lunar rocks the female vulture seizes
> The skeleton of love, and the rocking of their
> interlock
> Confuses categories, convulses shape, rocks the
> rocks.

The tragedy and chaos of birth are thus realized as a macabre union; the physical act which brings the innocent babe, as well as the castaways, to the shade is morbidly destructive and disgusting. Life is punishment for the spirit, caught like a butterfly in sunlight: "Spreadeagled like the full length mirror,/Pinioned like brilliant butterfly,/Fixed through gold axle on the Ixion sky."

The babe's condition prompts the overwhelming question: "What cause/Flings the star babe after the flying star?" The line reveals not only man's meteor-like existence—his life as a wild flight determined by some heavenly pitcher—but also the dynamic universe's own instability, where the thing toward which the babe moves is in rapid flight too and is in fact only another flying star. Although the metaphysical question is indeed very old, the suggestion of relative and rapid movement as a condition of life is influenced by theories of modern science. The creator of the modern world must be a paradox of love and destruction: "Who is

the parent of the innumerable plant . . . whose appalling paroxysm of love" engenders nature's instruments of death, the "lightning shoots?" Are the clouds and sun ("gold eyeball") features of
the "unknown face?"

The primarily destructive god of the world of flux is the "Blood
god" (Stanza 9) whose blood returns to him and who is omnis-
cient regarding his own carnal affairs; if he is not carnivorous, he
must at least be called the god of passion, of man's sexual nature,
of the libido. He is preeminently anthropomorphic, the god of *this*
world in the individual consciousness (or unconscious) which reflects the whole shade. "No secret move/Disturbing blood but to
god transfuses./Wherever he lies in what removed ward/The kiss
of acts registers red on his lips." Ironically, however, not to act
defies God's laws. The babe in the womb world becomes thus
sinful, hanging "in a vacuum,/suspended like a world between
pull of opposed forces,/The downward demon pull, the upward
angel." What could be more contradictory and painful than such a
conclusion? The babe is guilty before he can prove himself innocent, caught between the claims of his duality. Thus he is subject
to original sin.

In Book II the search motif continues. "Looking for the long
lost upward . . . the vision," the speaker seeks answers as to our
origin. The birth trauma itself and the growth of the babe are
interwoven with evocations of the futility of life where living is
dying; the soul is imprisoned in the body; and the desperate man,
comparable perhaps to the lost violent souls of "The Hollow
Men," goes with "excessive velocity" to death. Book II records the
psychological history of Faustian striving which ends in the disintegration of the aspirant and forces him to identify with all men,
who are, after all, mortal.

Book III takes up the journey through the childhood of the *enfant terrible:*

> The boy bud springing from the maternal tree
> Still senses the original blood, the bud or deer
> Drinks from the red jet of the female thigh.
> The doped colt on the Caliente course
> Running amok is the blood baited boy.
> I see him in the centre of destruction,

> The screaming cat, the tin can dog,
> The frog dissected, the one-eyed calf,
> The thrush in vice.

The violent boy, baited by blood, indulges his destructive nature. To the center of destruction are juxtaposed suggestions of sadistic boyhood tricks: making a cat scream, tying a tin can on a dog's tail, dissecting a frog, putting out the eye of a calf, watching "The thrush in vice."

The "upward" is long lost in this dream of the fallen condition (Stanza 3); the "long lost upward" which descends is the remembrance of fragments of early youth. But the young domestic cock (to Jung a symbol of libido) becomes in his fourteenth year a man: "The bleeding cockerel tethered to the tree/At the fourteenth fall achieves metamorphosis." All of the fragments of a violent adolescence go to make up the birth of the man, and the emergence is another birth trauma. In Jungian terms, the poem might be said to record the transformation of the libido through the two periods of transition to the adult sexual function—"*the epoch of suckling and the epoch of the displaced rhythmic activity.*" [7] Book III reveals the displaced activity of undirected sexual energy.

In Book IV the persona seems, however, to have discovered the channel for his energies. The young man, who asks for poetic inspiration, says "render me/O summer zephyr, the nightingale's bough." He hopes, no doubt, to emulate Yeats' changeless artist of Byzantium. He asks the wind to "Load up my flower with plenitude of sorrow,/The pollen that like pain produces pearls"; suffering is necessary for the tragic beauty of poetry, for the pearl "Makes fall the word from my hand." Furthermore, he wishes for "the note of love" and for "The evening vivid with mythologies."

As an adult, a late blooming flower ("Growing chrysanthemum"), recalling the birth trauma ("The autumn odor of the ninemonth horror"), the speaker finally asks for inspiration ("electrify my tepid heart") and for a more realistic point of view —"The starved figures of obligation . . . the thinning elongated guts of fact,/The Derbyshire starvation, the Welsh hell" (Stanza 2). The state of the macrocosm begins to impinge upon the speaker. He recalls "winter women of margarine and tears"

(Stanza 5) whom he associates with his mother, "more maternal than summer," from whom he "learned that love/Draws the lost and lonely toward the warmth." He asks them to

> Inhabit my word and render it deep and terrible
> Searching for something, probing for the soul.
> O winter women, expert in lamenting,
> Instruct my speech in the accent of despair—
> When I descend, I shall find nothing there.

The poet inverts the approach of the poets of the 1930's by invoking the miners' wives not primarily to present or sympathize with their problems, but to use them as symbols of his personal dilemma. The "million loss" (Stanza 7) is not that of "The fatal queue waiting at the minehead" (Stanza 6); it is his own. He sacrifices himself for the sake of discovering his soul: "I tear my guts out on the platform/Or rummage in my stomach with bloody hands/To catch the mole or bird."

The symbols for soul are reiterated when the "bowels' cave" becomes "My subterranean canals of love Venetian" (Stanza 11); voluptuous love is associated with Venice, "My lovely gondolas. . . . But where are the birds, the Mark pigeons" of St. Mark's Cathedral, the symbols of soul? He appeals to them with "O bosom birds,/Violate me with your violence!" The violations described earlier were physical, purposeless, or masochistic; but now the violation is the martyrdom of the body to release the soul. Like John Donne in "Batter my heart, three personed God," Barker insists that the soul present itself in violent strength, that it "spring/Like the blood babe at my feet." The original libidinal energy may be said to be transferred, as Jung puts it, "to an analogy. The libido is taken away from its proper place and transferred to another substratum." [8]

Although the speaker desires mystical transport, the soul, which might be his vehicle to Identity, is lost. Book V treats the *ubi sunt* theme; "intimations of immortality" are recollected from early childhood. The speaker formerly wondered why the symbols for liberated spirit could sing in a degenerate land. In the past, the symbols for imagination and soul, unspoiled by the suburban degeneracy of Babylonian Ealing, behaved joyfully, almost like Psalm singers who clap their hands and make a joyful noise or like

Yeats' artist's soul which could "clap hands and sing," despite the sensual world. The Psalm singer sat down and wept by the waters of Babylon as he remembered Zion and all that his homeland meant to him in captivity. In the suburbs of proud London, condemned for iniquity, the symbols of spiritual values could in the past "sometimes" be heard. But the present is different.

The innocent child could hear the music of the spheres, but the adult of Book V "in the Dorset/Remove" [9] cannot, though once in "Ealing Common" he heard it. While he tries to fix upon his soul, he is distracted by the image of physical desire which he has not transcended; he holds women in his "bowels." In considering what to do with life in the absence of the visionary imagination, synonymous with the soul, the young poet contemplates Romantic "suicide in the Bay of Naples" and the offerings of "the chaos of experience." From fragmentary associations,

> Vague design takes shape,
> The Italian lady conforms to temptation,
> The shade of Milton instructs me in ambition,
> The letter from Italy is always arriving
> Suggesting suicide in the Tyrrhenian,
> The fall from it all, secession, sleep.

The three images conform roughly to the medieval temptations of the world (ambition), the devil (suicide), and the flesh (the Italian lady).

Without the visionary imagination, the self-centered point of view is likely to produce inversion and madness. Book VI treats the disaster of egoism, the calamiterror which is the turning point and climax of the poem. Barker describes the apocalyptic moment when the persona realizes his complete selfishness and the total inversion of his values. The experience is very much like that Pascal described in the *Pensées*—"We burn with desire to find solid ground and an ultimate sure foundation whereon to build a tower leading to the Infinite. But our whole groundwork cracks; and the earth opens to abysses." [10] The life cycle whose end is like its beginning promises no achievement or fulfillment; all aspects of time— past, present, and future—collapse into this appalling recognition of failure. With the universe thus closing in on him, the young narcissus begins to see, however, that his world is distorted. When the ego becomes its own object, the individual experiences a terrible calamity bordering on the disintegration of personality.

But discovery precedes growth. The adult must realize that he is not the center of existence. Youth, wholly egocentric, is unhappy because it cannot assimilate the world, "this indigestion,/ The world swelling in his guts." The poem is the act of expulsion, the expression of nausea: "I vomit./This is the act I now execute." The unpleasant image expresses something of the nature of the poetic technique of *Calamiterror*.

As Blake's disciple, the young man with spiritual indigestion apprehended the universe with himself as center; but, when his vision of Blake falls (Stanza 12), he recognizes the importance of "external fact." Blake, "larger than my Lincolnshire mountain/ . . . fell." The force of this catastrophic experience is conveyed by a comparison to Krakatoa, whose terrific explosion in 1883 blew up part of the volcanic island on which it was located, changed its shape, and formed a new island. This simile is reinforced by "like the/Fist shooting out of the box," to indicate the explosive nature of the recognition that mysticism is not the way. But the change is paradoxical, both sudden and gradual and inevitable, "like the gradual/Appearance of morning at morning." The boy Egyptian king, Tutankhamen, who restored the warlike Amon as god and whose splendid tomb is synonymous with empire and social stability, vaguely connotes the richness of an experience which means a change of gods:

> William Blake was larger than my Lincolnshire
> mountain
> When like my mountain fell, I heard the cata-
> strophic
> Fragments of his torso breaking past me, it was
> The object of the physical world breaking on me
> Like Krakatoa like Krakatoa like the
> Fist shooting out of the box like the gradual
> Appearance of morning at morning like Tutankhamen
> Carefully divesting itself in public places.

Somewhat paradoxically divesting himself of what Barker considered to be Blake's mysticism, the persona puts on the robes of the prophet. His vision is composed of the sounds of the external world:

> I achieved apocalypse—hearing slowly the sounds
> Again which my ears had made their own music.
> I heard first the Rhondda choral echo up the valley
> Trying to find god's ear, I heard the presage
> Ironically rumbling along the Channel, war:
> The ancestral voice, the ancestral voice. And
> I saw in a fog of gas Mr. Baldwin orating:
> We must repair the deficiencies of our forces.
> I heard three women weeping in Irun's ruins.

The women who had been inside himself become the mourners for the plight of Spain; Irun, a city in Northern Spain staunchly defended by the Loyalists who burned it before it fell to the Fascists in 1936, becomes a contemporary symbol of Loyalist defense against tyranny.

The awful vision of social unrest grows more vivid in Stanza 14. Newsboys strike. German, English, French and Russian newspapers recount "Instances of hate, of insult, aggravation," while the working classes of the mining areas of Great Britain continue their hymns. At Salisbury Cathedral the saints try to shut out the chaotic sounds "with cottonwool in their ears." Their attempt to escape reality reminds the speaker of his own behavior: "I remembered with shame my own music./The splitting of the central pillar like aural lightning,/I felt it crack my abdomen, the world."

Here "world" is rightly ambiguous for the purposes of the poem; the political world with the antecedent "it" cracks the abdomen of the microcosm; and the world, in apposition to abdomen, is the little world of self. With this birth trauma, social consciousness is born. "The splitting of the central pillar" is the breaking of the axis of the egocentric universe. The simile "like aural lightning" reveals synaesthetically the effect the apocalyptic sounds have upon the self-centered world. The ambiguities of the last lines of Book VI appropriately assert the equivocal nature of the relationship between microcosm and macrocosm within the confines of the individual consciousness, which is, of course, the setting of *Calamiterror*.

Having achieved awareness of the world, the speaker is prepared to celebrate his discovery. Book VII, like books I and II, begins with the contradictory description of birth—"born upward breaking from heaven downward," but now "break . . . downward" has a new connotation. We remember Blake falling and the physical world breaking on the persona. The influence nature can have upon the newborn creature is indeed great. The book begins:

> What when born upward breaking from heaven downward
> Brilliantly glittering the new-born eye, firing
> The flame of grace, what when descending on the babe
> Terrible in the toil of original sin, shines, showers,
> Cleanses, charges, redeems the demand divine?

Although the Hopkins-like line seems to require the Holy Spirit as answer, the new-born Romantic finds his answer in the *spiritus mundi,* "O world, my white breasted, my cruelly crowned. . . ." The speaker praises the world while gradually disclosing the awful fact of her decline; she moves in time, a "westward wanderer." Now the swan's symbolic value is enlarged; the world sings its swan song. But the dark is at least not the darkness of the womb world. The swan's one note "Awoke me in the bower of the womb; I rose/And saw her passing on the dark westward stream,/The myriad of human struggling at her breast."

Book VIII takes up the motif of the world sailing on the "Time-Thames" of flux. Growth and decay become aspects of the same cycle. The tidal surge and recession of the wave represent the continual resurgence of life, "The wave approaching and the wave returning." The book is organized in terms of the life cycle treated in the first seven books. Stanza 8 begins by repeating the first line of Stanza 1 and then variations on the theme. The poet lists aspects of life lived in a world of change:

> The wave approaching and the wave returning,
> The opening stone and the worm eternal,
> The animal of agony at the groin
> Fighting to burst the sex bag of skin;
> The giant I, crucified to my spine,
> Who stretches and crushes me—I suffer
> Seeing the bruises burgeon along the body
> Blossom to bring the suffocator rose.

But in Book IX the ambivalent attitude toward death is recognized implicitly as unhealthy, for it is another form of calamiterror and of self-centeredness. Book IX presents the recoil from self;

and the free, integrated personality leaves behind the infantile ego, willing him the fragments that represent faulty transformations to false love, ambition, suicide, and all of the wandering selves pursued in *Calamiterror* which are now seen to be extensions of the fragmented, unfulfilled personality. Like the phoenix arising from its own funeral pyre, like the beetle shedding his shell, like the snake shedding his skin, the integrated personality rises the same in substance, but radically different, only to become once more involved in birth pangs, born now to a social conscience: "I rose and felt the throes of Spain."

Book X turns to consider impending political catastrophe in Spain and England. The emergence of the free self is comparable to the emergence of the free world, symbolized by Spain: "See how she stands,/Her Madrid middle growing vague with ravage,/Labouring to let out liberty, with the rat and the rot at her heart." The speaker is reminded of Irun and Asturias, the setting of the bloody 1934 miners' uprising in Spain, one of the many violent and unequal battles between Loyalists and "the Franco gangs." The political man tries to wring from Loyalist defeats promise of ultimate victory: "It is already time to triumph, for tears and blood like time/Take tears and blood as time takes time to make good." This is a wordy way of asserting that the end justifies the means. The idea conveyed is something like Churchill's later expression of the power of blood, sweat and tears.

The final stanza of *Calamiterror* completes the poet's vision of an agonized world:

> I see the swan's breast run like the pelican's red
> To feed the crowded myriad her human,
> I see the large parasites that dilate like leech
> Torn, with war and agony, from my mother world's front.
> But the whippoorwill wends his way through the Wyoming
> woods
> When the leopard, lying low, awaits, or the lion
> Roars. And my mother world, with bomb holes in her
> bosom,
> Goes gradually on, with the myriad of me at her breast.

The return to the personal consideration is necessary, for *Calamiterror* depends for its overall effect upon a kind of cumulative synthesis. Images of one stanza, its correspondences, and comparisons become meaningful in terms of other stanzas, so that all parts of the poem are finally revealed as interdependent. "The myriad of me" means more than the selves of the microcosm; it affirms the meaning toward which the whole poem has progressed —that the individual has achieved integration in associating himself with the fate of "the crowded myriad her human." "Me" is Everyman. The growth from selfish egoism to social vision is the process of development from youth to maturity. Moreover, in terms of the cyclical development of *Calamiterror*, it would have been inconsistent not to evoke a symbol of the personality in the conclusion. Out of the birth cycles which comprise the poem comes the child of the world, whose love of nature has led to love of man.

III   *The Dialectical Method*

The treatment of birth is the clue to the relationship between form and subject matter; it makes the two in a very real sense inseparable. Underlying *Calamiterror* is a cyclical view of individual and universal history—the dialectical method of creation that Barker described in 1938 in "A Note on the Dialectics of Poetry." The reiterations of the birth trauma, which at first reading seem tautological, are actually an expression of a basically dynamic concept of life as transformation. Each change in the growth of the individual from infancy to maturity involves the violent expulsion from the known to the unknown. The womb-wish lurking behind connotations of a constantly recurring birth process is the inverse expression of the calamiterror. But the poem illustrates that one is always expelled into a world where, in psychological terms, the libido wars to assert itself; or the Blakean selfhood wars with its spectre; or, the Yeatsian self with its mask. The integration of personality is possible only when these opposites are reconciled.

The imagery of the perpetual conflict is repetitive, but not because the poet cannot control his material. The technique is a graphic illustration of symbolic transformation as one might understand it from reading Jung's *The Psychology of the Unconscious*. The basic birth symbol is transformed to represent each phase of the development of personality. Physiological birth comes finally to stand for emergence of social consciousness.

Meaning is never caught up in a single, precise image; instead, it develops from a string of images which have a common quality or which elucidate aspects of a larger concept or emotion. The technique bears something in common with the cataloguing of Milton or of Walt Whitman. It can be justified because *Calamiterror* is basically a stream-of-consciousness work designed to reflect and to reveal the fragmentation of subjective experience. The technique, at bottom, associative, can be illustrated with a typical stanza. Stanza 1, Book IX, clearly refers to the narcissism basic to the "I" whose

> Centre of the heart
> Shoots forth a hand pointing towards mirrors.
> And when I look I see myself embroiled like
> The Egyptian corpse in images of self.
> I feel the heavy towelling of space
> Wound round my active corpse which is alive
> Like bug in vacuum only in itself.
> I scratch the itch of self to make it swell.

Like a mummy, the speaker is wrapped up in "images of self." The winding cloths of the mummy suggest "the heavy towelling. . . ." The tomb in which the "active corpse" is alive is paralleled to "bug in vacuum," alive only in the vault of self. The transition from "bug" to "scratch the itch" indicates that "I" is both subject and object—all things—tormentor and tormented, pursuer and pursued—in the microcosm. "I scratch the itch of self to make it swell" refers to the bugbite, the self-search itself and the masturbatory magnification of ego that has constituted the poem. The "swelling" is the enlargement of the poem.

In many sections, especially in the later books of *Calamiterror*, subjective and objective worlds are willfully mixed. The highly allusive style represents a great change from the 1935 volume. Place references give the individual's search in the microcosm geographical location, usually narrowly within the vicinity of London where the speaker is no doubt actually wandering—in Twickenham, Richmond, Ealing, or near the Thames at Sonning. Rural English counties, like Shropshire, qualify aspects of the free spirit; others, like Northumberland and Lancashire signify economic distress. Symbols for release are associated with the country and those for slavery to materialism and capitalism with the industrial and mining areas. In early books geographical allusions refer to internal conflict; as the speaker achieves social vision, they become symbols of social and economic conflict. As the poem develops, allusions become less insular; it moves from the womb of London to its environs to the geography of England, and finally to Spain.

IV *Mythopoeic Technique*

Although geographical allusions establish a setting in space, others back up the basically dynamic concept of time which dominates *Calamiterror*. When at the beginning of Book IV the growing poet asks his muse to "bring/The evening vivid with mythologies," he refers to an important constituent of the poem, itself vivid with mythology. The mythological references and symbols strengthen the cyclical pattern and indicate that the central consciousness sees himself related to the archetypal patterns of the collective unconscious.

The myths most pervasive are those of ascent. The Phaeton story is implied in Book II where the celestial aspect of the newborn babe aspires to return from whence it came, only to be forced by a fall into the chaos of the human condition: "Then the heavenly curvetting through heaven,/The bird, the butterfly the aeronaut,/The final bone falls like the Indian boy." The simile probably refers to Phaeton who went to India, region of sunrise, where he began his calamitous trip through the heavens in an effort to assert his divine parentage. Images of attempts at flight suggest Phaeton, Icarus, and any number of rebellious heroes. The myths describe the eternal aspirations of youth "Seeking a place and time he does not know." The recurring symbol of the salamander is related to Phaeton, who would inherit from Apollo the eternal element of fire, the soul. Barker's persona wants to be "Runaway rainbow," although, in words appropriate for Barker's "Daedalus," he says, "at my feet falls the burnt out fragment/ The finger or the face sheered off clean."

Polar to the myth of ascent is the narcissus archetype of descent into the waters of self; for much of *Calamiterror* explores the implications of narcissism. In Book VI (Stanza 3), when the speaker begins to realize that his world has been distorted, he exhorts others who wander in nature to "Throw up no mountain featured with self's face. If "you" admire "the bright mask/Suspended through   the   depths . . . down/Internally   and   eternally drowned you go. I know." References to Narcissus, Hylas, Apollo, and Ixion people the poem.

When the individual's history records the struggle for release from the body, when the individual is self-contained, a world unto himself, references to myth underlie the imagery. As the speaker comes to think of himself less as a hermaphroditic god, he uses fewer references to Greek legend. Throughout the poem, however, allusions to Christianity establish correspondence between the sacred and the profane to enunciate the central tension between spiritual aspirations and the claims of the body and physical life.

V *The Continuity of Literary Experience*

The mythopoeic technique extends and universalizes the individual experience of *Calamiterror*. Direct or implied allusions to poets and poetry are equally important: they produce the sense of the continuity of the poet's experience. In Book V, for example, the aspiring mystic has a preliminary vision, brief and less significant than the one of Blake in Book VI; the first vision reminds him of death by water, like Shelley's, and "instructs me in ambition." In Book VIII, this ambition becomes "Milton nibbling like a mouse" (Stanza 5). Although Milton is only an allegorical synonym for ambition, Blake is the symbol for the mystic and a focal point for the whole poem.

The turning point in the persona's dark night of spirit acknowledges the debt. Stanzas 9 through 12 of Book VI present Blake as the central vision in the apocalyptic experience of the calamiterror: "I saw/The figure of William Blake bright and large/Hung over the Thames at Sonning. I had not had this." The vision is almost like a Blake engraving. The poet explains that he had thus far apprehended the external universe as a materialist, "Acknowledging the element of matter," and not wholly as a mystic. He had not discovered his archetype: "I had not acknowledged this,/I had not encountered prototype." The speaker realizes that Blake too had "worlds and worlds in his abdomen,/And his bosom innumerably enpeopled with all birds." The vision implies Blake's debt to Swedenborg, "labouring like a dream in his stomach," and Barker's debt to Blake, "myself the minor bird on the bough." Significantly, however, this image suggests that Yeats was the major and Barker a minor disciple of Blake. The speaker admits that he has been the apostle of Blake, who is "Absolute, glittering, actual and gold,"—the pattern of the visionary of apocalyptic literature and the speaker's Ideal.

Through Blake, then, the poet comes upon revelation; the apocalypse is paradoxical in that he apprehends not eternity but the real world. He realizes that objective reality will make of subjective chaos an ordered universe. When he recognizes the importance of "external fact," his vision of Blake falls (Stanza 12). This catastrophe for subjectivism comes about as "Fragments of his torso breaking past me" is juxtaposed to "It was/The object of the physical world breaking on me." The fall of introverted mysticism makes the young man into a poet-prophet who is, ironically, like Blake.

Barker's use of geographical references to give internal drama spatial dimensions and to remind us of "external fact" is similar to the technique Blake used in his prophecies, particularly in *Jerusalem*. In Book X the first stanza derives from Blake's "A Song of Liberty" in *The Marriage of Heaven and Hell:*

1. The Eternal Female groan'd! it was heard over
     all the Earth.
2. Albion's coast is sick silent: the American
     meadows faint!
3. Shadows of Prophecy shiver along by the lakes
     and the rivers and mutter across the oceans:
     "France, rend down thy dungeon.
4. "Golden Spain, burst the barriers of old Rome.

Barker places much the same song in a modern context:

The English coast shivers and the American meadow faints;
The Rhone and the Rhine run mellowing with promised horror;
The Welsh mountain weeps and the Cumberland fell weeps;
London lies like a huge rot along the Thames, and Rome
Roars. O Spain, my golden red, she tears the rot out,
The Franco gangs that furrow in her heart. See how she stands,
Labouring to let out liberty, with the rat and the rot at her heart.

Barker's language, tone, use of personification, and the subject of impending upheaval against tyranny are remarkably like Blake's. No wonder Barker called upon Blake as the catalyst to this final liberation song. The shade of modern life is like Blake's "genera-tion," and the god of contemporary chaos is like his Jehovah, a wrathful and destructive "Blood god" who is Nobodaddy.

Barker espouses the Blakean idea that action in itself is good and that "Sin is not to act." Even his treatment of man as a dualis-tic combination of warring opposites—the superhuman and the subhuman, energy and reason, spirit and flesh—may be traced to Blake, who believed, as Barker does at the start of *Calamiterror*, in the god-man. Barker's opposed forces and the whole concep-tion of his poem are related to Blake's contraries, without which there is "no progression" and to the reiteration of Blake's ideas as Barker found them in Yeats. Barker's babe is itself a marriage of heaven and hell. Blake's theory that "one portion of being is the Prolific; the other the Devouring" is part of the total fabric of *Calamiterror*.

The poem progresses from Blakean monism, which insists upon dualities within one entity, to Wordsworthian dualism, which ac-cepts the separation and interplay, rather than the identification of subject and object. The development and certain ideas and ex-periences explored are surely influenced by Wordsworth. Although *Calamiterror* makes no specific reference to the author of *The Prelude, The Recluse,* and *Tintern Abbey,* he is present in the background. Barker's subject is, like Wordsworth's, the growth of the poet's mind.

"Introductory Stanzas" (Stanza 4) indicates that the past, pres-ent, and future become substantial as we become involved in life: "as we grow older/Achieving mass . . . we become the shade." Infant innocence is blotted out. Man "ascends . . . through/ The wreckage of his perfection,/Burdened with the ball of world" (II, st. 10). Barker's babe, like Wordsworth's Youth, is "by the vision attended"; but, in Wordsworth's words, "Shades of the prison-house begin to close/Upon the growing Boy . . ./At length the Man perceives it [the vision] die away,/And fade into the light of common day." [11] Barker, like Wordsworth, becomes a realist.

The modern Romantic remembers the visionary gleam; in Book V, Barker asks very much the same question that Wordsworth asks with "Whither is fled the visionary gleam/Where is it now, the glory and the dream?" Barker asks "What have I done that takes my birds away?" Wordsworth recalls, however, his vision in

"To the Cuckoo" where he describes a search like Barker's but a conclusion tranquillized by memory. Barker writes that his birds "sometimes . . . reappear . . . tantalizing, divine, ephemeral, immediately gone./Leaving the whisp of a feather, tinted with tongue,/Lying like an epitaph in the curve of my hand."

Like the Wordsworth of Book I of *The Prelude,* Barker's persona wanders alone in a rural setting. Wordsworth's boy indulges in relatively innocent activities such as killing a bird, plundering a nest, or stealing a boat; Barker's Cain figure is more destructive (cf. Book III, Stanza 1). In Book VI, the calamiterror seems at first to be the discipline of fear Wordsworth described in *The Prelude* when he also imaginatively projected his fear into the mountain which became

> a huge peak, black and huge
> As if with voluntary power instinct
> And growing still in stature the grim shape
> Towered up between me and the stars, and still
> For so it seemed, with purpose of its own
> And measured motionlike a living thing
> Strode after me. (I, 11.378–85)

Life in nature disciplined Wordsworth because his imagination attributed significance to natural objects which revealed states of the young poet's mind; Barker's experience is similar:

> Meandering abroad in the Lincolnshire meadows day
> Day and day a month perhaps, lying at night lonely,
> The early September evening administering a mystery,
> The moon executing its wavering sleight of hand, I sense the
> Advent of the extraordinary event, the calamiterror,
> Turn and encounter the mountain descending upon me—
> The moment of terror flashes like dead powder
> Revealing the features of the mass as mine. (VI, Stanza 1)

Rather than project his fears into nature, Barker identifies himself with it and with the fear it represents. Where Wordsworth saw similarities, Barker, like Blake, sees identities.

In *The Prelude,* Wordsworth pays tribute to Nature as "Leading to Love of Man"; Barker devotes Book VII to celebrating love of nature as "my mother/World" before indicating his newborn sympathy for mankind. Both poets, as Wordsworth put it, underwent "that bursting forth/Of sympathy, inspiring and inspired";[12] and their "thought by slow gradations had been drawn / To humankind." [13] Wordsworth recollects his early enthusiasm for the French Revolution; Barker centers his sympathies on Loyalist Spain. Wordsworth anticipated Barker when he wrote:

> Not Chaos, not
> The darkest pit of lowest Erebus,
> Nor aught of blinder vacancy, scooped out
> By help of dreams, can breed such fear and awe
> As fall upon us when we look
> Into our Minds, into the Mind of Man
> My haunt, and the main region of my
> Song.[14]

The continuity of religious experience, or rather the ironic contrast between past and present religious experience, is revealed by allusions to George Herbert's "The Collar" and "The Pulley." Barker makes of Herbert's "good cable" a hangman's noose. His speaker tries to use simple machines—pulley and lever—to start himself in motion in the right direction, but the truth is that "The rope of god throttling me was my guts" (IX, Stanza 2).

Overtones of Spenser and Milton inform Stanza 6, Book IX. When the regenerated man emerges from the womb of the former self, "The bowels I burst from" lying askew about him are also the offspring of the selfish microcosm, coming to life like the brood in the burst womb of the monster in Book I of Spenser's *Faerie Queene*. Spenser's loathsome details are suggested when Barker treats a similar instance of offspring "murdering its parent." From the verbal opulence of Spenser the stanza rapidly moves to suggest Milton's satan who, from an incestuous relationship with sin, produced death: "He loved himself so much that the act of love/ Made with himself, gave him as hybrid, death." Barker echoes predecessors of Romanticism whose dynamic treatment of moral issues and "fine writing" he emulates.

Although style and content of *Calamiterror* are developed against the background of English literature, it is a prëeminently modern poem whose political ideology echoes that of the Pylon poets and whose use of conscious control over the material of the unconscious foreshadows the work of poets of the New Apocalypse. It is salutary that the associative technique is influenced by Eliot. Like Eliot (and most modern poets), Barker is distressed by the sterility and complacency of modern society. In Book V, when Barker envisions, in contrast to modern degeneracy, a past where spiritual activity was possible, we are reminded of *The Waste Land.*

Book VIII, which conveys the concept of time underlying the poem, is, generally speaking, about the same subject as the *Four Quartets;* the first of Eliot's poems, "Burnt Norton" (1935), begins with a Greek epigraph from Heraclitus, the second fragment of which is translated "The way upward and downward are one and the same." This verticle expression of the "wave approaching and wave returning" is related to Barker's paradoxical "born upward breaking. . . . downward," which appears and reappears in *Calamiterror.* Both Barker and Eliot show a special concern for cyclical history and express it in terms of the Heraclitean paradox. Barker does not, however, see time in its relationship to eternity in a philosophical or orthodox religious manner. Everything in Barker's poem is centered in a single personality. And although Barker, like Eliot, uses archetypal patterns, it is important to note that his growth is to a social, not to a religious center.

Ultimately, *Calamiterror,* in its strong emphasis on man's sexual nature and on the birth process, is most clearly analogous to the early poetry of Dylan Thomas. Barker also dreams his genesis; but he emerges as a more literary, derivative poet than Thomas. Like the Welshman, however, he sees the boys of summer "singing among the summer horror" (II, Stanza 3). For him too the splitting belly of repeated life and death begins and ends in darkness. The physiological and Freudian implications, the startling associations, the basic paradox and fundamental vocabulary suggest why critics began to pair Barker and Thomas.

Compression combined with repetition contribute to Barker's daring experiment, which, like *Finnegans Wake,* explores the limits of language, internalizing the drama to a point beyond which it could not go and still communicate. In Barker's poem, opposites are reconciled as the speaker emerges from the shadow. This vivid and unusual chronical of subjective search records what Dylan Thomas described as the theme of his own poetry —one man's struggle from darkness to light.

CHAPTER 4

Lament and Triumph *and After*:
The Unacknowledged Legislator

IN *Calamiterror* Barker became the poet-*engagée;* in *Lament and Triumph* (1940) a change in attitude and style emerges. "Resolution of Dependence" describes the determination to fix "on the facts," and it provides a key to Barker's approach to most of the middle poems. The poem is an apologia for an "absurd and abysmal past." The title alludes, of course, to Wordsworth's "Resolution and Independence"; and, like Wordsworth, Barker asserts his freedom from egocentricity and its correlative "despondence and madness." After the extreme subjectivity of the past, Barker must choose either "a suicide or a resolution." Barker creates a scene in which an old man teaches a young man to face life. In the setting of his poem, Barker places Wordsworth, "Obviously emulating the old man of the mountain moor," on the "outskirts of the noisy crowd." The speaker confronts his vision of the Romantic poet, a father confessor through whom "the violent gestures of the individualist" can be "absolved."

I *Resolving to Fix on Facts*

Where *Calamiterror* was hallucinatory and internalized, "Resolution of Dependence" objectifies vision. But the vision is a device of the poem, not the poem itself, Wordsworth is a character distinct from the persona, and imaginary conversation is treated in realistic terms. The style—discursive, direct, almost prosaic—is entirely appropriate, and Barker uses conversational understatement such as "Remarkable I reflected that after all it is him." It treats vision with ironic detachment: "The acute superstition that Wordsworth is after all dead/Should have succeeded in keeping him quiet and cold."

In straightforward syntax with clear allegorical implication, Barker describes "the crowd returning from amusements,/The

Bournemouth Pavilion, or the marvelous gardens,/The Palace of Solace, the Empyrean. . . ." The poem combines something very near to objective reporting (of, however, imaginary experience) with the use of private symbols for aspects of the past. When Wordsworth questions the speaker regarding the loss of individualism, the speaker affirms the "loss of my charms"—the symbols of an unrealistic life: the "bird" of youthful spirit, "the penis water pistol" of adolescent sex, and the "tulip trumpet" of ineffectual prophecy.

Simile informs the new style, helping to assimilate some arch, almost metaphysical comparisons: "The accumulation of year and year like calendar"; "the passing people, like Saint Vitus, averted their eyes"; "I saw his eyes like a bent pin searching for eyes/To grip and catch"; "it is ghosts,/Trailing, like snails, an excrement of signs." Alliteration ("The paradise pets I kept in my pocket") is still a favorite device. The long, free-verse line and a predominant vocabulary of statement, without rhyme, create unity of meaning and technique. Although the excitement of earlier poems is missing, this one should not be "susceptible of innumerable interpretations" (Stanza 7). Barker, aware of his early reputation for obscurity, now wants to communicate.

The new attitude is again apparent in "Allegory of the Adolescent and the Adult." In it the theme, developed in "Resolution of Dependence" out of a single dramatic situation, is reworked in terms of a quest or a journey. The allegory itself moves from a "gay mood" of adolescence, up "hills anticipating the strange" to the summits and "sorrow" of maturity. The early search for identity—and "for a worse wonder, a rare one"—is remembered; but now the passionate expectation of some "miraculous catastrophe" makes way, as youth does, for the maturer realization that the real miracle is to accept the world as it is. From this hilltop at journey's end it is clear that

> The world is my wonder, where the wind
> Wanders like wind, and where the rock is
> Rock. And man and woman flesh on a dream.
> I look from my hill with the woods behind,
> And time, a sea's chaos, below.

II   *Responding to Impending War*

To stand in the world's wind during the 1930's could mean only one thing: "In our time," Thomas Mann had written, "the destiny of man presents its meaning in political terms." Anxieties and discontents—social, political, and almost universal—were gathering into the storm that would bring that decade to a close. Barker's middle poetry in *Lament and Triumph* and *Selected Poems* (1941) is largely a record of his reaction to the events leading up to World War II.

The poems in *Lament and Triumph* are more often lamentations than triumphal odes. The title might seem misleading but not when we recall Barker's alleged triumph over egocentricity and his 1940 pronouncement that all poems are elegies wherein "the real grief is the possibility of joy." [1] The title poem establishes a mood of ambivalence; it mourns spiritual collapse, yet insists on the ironic triumph of speaking truth: "There is one way to restore this wreckage:/I'm Einstein and Aeschylus and I'm Truth—/Keep me in mind and suffer ruth for me." Accepting modern science and relativity, the tragic dimensions of art, and Truth itself as an absolute, Barker nevertheless feels that the world can literally be "reformed" by the poet as unacknowledged legislator.

This poem, like many others in the volume, is as much about the poet's reaction to suffering as it is about suffering itself. Like Atlas, he feels the weight of the world on his shoulders, "The broken pillars and arches on my shoulder. . . ." But he identifies himself as the microcosm of mankind: "I am myself those ones/On whom a world has fallen its tons." The assertion in "Lament and Triumph" that the individual suffers the sores of the broken and the fallen anticipates the subject matter of many of the poems of this period; many, like this one, perform a cathartic function: "Cleansing their mankind's sores with words of anger,/Laving their hurt with my heart's pollen."

The individual faces the bitter truth of impending war in "Triumphal Ode Mcmxxxix"—the title itself being an ironic comment on the occurrences of 1939. Nature, in the Keatsian richness of the end of summer, is alive with suggestions of the blood, sweat, and tears to come: "I hear the tree weep/Its sweat of tears"; "summer sheds its blood"; "Autumn comes over and renders into flame/The general green," while ironically the south wind seems to speak of love. Nature itself is changed by war: the Thames becomes "an aorta of war"; "Temperate is the weather of all other worlds,/But ours is red at morning." Barker foresees the ugly future where hate will cause countless deaths, for

> This is the year that must be memorable
> Not for its crop of corn or its fine weather,
> Not for its anniversaries, but rather
> Memorable for the terrible star in the South,
> The badge of war.

III   A Prophetic Vision

The poet oftens wears the robes of a prophet in *Lament and Triumph*. One of his most ambitious efforts, "Vision of England '38," is a lyric of social protest, a vision which operates from a central experience to a circumference wide in social significance. From his bed in Brighton the speaker had a waking vision (Part I: "I lay in bed not sleeping not dreaming . . . I saw the imperial procession . . . I heard voices"); he arose to stand by the sea, much as Arnold did in "Dover Beach," for a nocturnal lamentation over social and political corruption (Part II: "I arose . . . near me the sea"); then he takes an imaginary journey to Northern England (Part III: "I ride my grief along the road . . . northward to Salisbury"), then farther North (Part IV: "I went towards Mount Rydal"), and finally to the East and South (Part IV: "Last in the Eastern Marshes I made a way . . . I saw you London astride the South").

Throughout the poem, Barker looks to the past to compare it implicitly to the present. Although he does not, like William Langland, "lay . . . in Malvern," he pleads as Piers Plowman did for the poor; and he envisions the tyranny of wealth—modern capitalism—over church and state. "The tremendous panoply of England" moving over his pillow is really a vision of the seven deadly sins, like Langland's or Spenser's:

> Not sleeping not dreaming I saw the imperial pro-
>   cession
> Flicker past my foot in postures of triumph or
>   violence;
> Some moved in shapes of gluttony or envy, others

> Rode pride like lions, and some bore their own
> flowers.

Into this parade of historical character comes a "word of hope,"
the skull of Shelley, crying like Hamlet's father's ghost for vengeance. Shelley's tear becomes the symbol for those such as Wat
Tyler and Robert Owen who suffered for social reform. It insists
that truth is possible and that close scrutiny of history will show a
"grander course" for life. Part II defines that course: history,
which provided deliverers for persecuted people, teaches the lesson. The persona contemplates the sad state of the imperial lion
"emaciated on capital rocks" and wishes for a hero, like Perseus, to
rescue an Andromeda chained because of her mother's pride. The
maternal past grieves:

> Cassiopeia wept. I felt her brilliant sympathy
> Falling upon me as I walked by the waves;
> I looked up at her outstretched arms in the sky
> Too far to reach me and too near for a grave.

As the mother weeps for her daughter (England), Perseus
merges with Saint George, whose heroic actions have proved fu-
tile because the Andromeda-Una "green girl" he rescued is being
seduced by modern capitalism:

> Then a saint walked up out of the sea,
> Dragging his death behind him like a boa
> He had a rusty sword and he said to me:
> 'I killed an enormous monster, but the brute
> Still rules England with its scales of gold.
> O my green girl given to the rape of the banker,
> The careerist politician and the vague thinker,
> Lie easy for one more night out in the cold.'

The rescuer turns his weapon over to the poet who finds that the
sword has been transformed into the pen, "The blue-blooded
point that bleeds a book." As the poet lies down beside the female
personification of England, he remembers that "Peace is dear, and
cannot be bought with sleep." Blake's little lamb, becomes a
"sheep," licks the wakeful dreamer to remind him that England
must be purged if a New Jerusalem is to be built.

While his vision is extended over the immensely sad land
"where only the ghosts are good," the persona sees Salisbury Cathedral as a symbol of dead faith and Alfred as a symbol of the
unified, peaceful kingdom of the past. Alfred points, however, to
the ugly present transformed by promises of violence:

> Manoeuvring over the broad water like gnats
> The naval seaplanes and the giant cruisers
> Spread their shadows over the boats and bathers
> Who played in Weymouth Bay among the shadows.
>
> Then I saw that they floated in blood and blossoms,
> The blood of the bathers, the blossoms of the boughs
> That made the boats: under the dreadnought bosoms
> Crushed and bruised under the huge bows.

The hero king cries for a defender and leader, for another father
for England, an Arthur.

When he remembers the "note of the swan who bleeds for her
purge," the swansong which is "the native music of contemporary
England," the poet asserts that revolutionary means are justified
by the end of peace: "though the purge shall bleed her in revolution. . . . If she achieves her perfect peace, it is the prize." The
crux of the problem is economic, a matter of "cash and credit":
"Everywhere here I see the larks of youth/Tethered to banks for a
debit." London is the monster Perseus-St. George would slay; and
the common people, the Andromeda-Una in distress:

> O London, Magnificent monster
>
> . . . .
> Where is the Cappadocian for that throat
> To cut the health and wealth of England loose?
> O Political Prince, from this rock release
> The national man and woman who groan.

The speaker appeals to King George to emulate past heroism. But,
although he petitions the monarch, he seems to believe that the
rise of the proletariat is inevitable:

> I see him rise sweating from the North,
> Up from the deep shaft or the steel yard:—

> He comes down not drummed or crowned or starred,
> But nevertheless inheritor of the earth.

> O equitable stars hasten that liberation!

The ideology is surely not simple political liberalism, nor is it orthodox Communism, despite its justification of proletarian revolution. The desire for a hero to rescue the working class betrays a faith in individual leadership similar to that of the Auden group, whose Marxism was also heterodox. Barker's Communism is tempered by nationality; his sympathy for revolution, by ardor for heroism and respect for the past.

Although the ideology is comparable to that of the Pylon group, the central message and the technique are influenced by Eliot. Barker contrasts past and present, blurs and blends symbols from Christian and pagan mythology, asserts that a quester is needed to restore the land, and uses the journey motif in a fashion that superficially resembles Eliot's strategy in *The Waste Land*. Nonetheless, the past Barker uses is one of his own choosing; the dream allegory setting and general allegorical implications suggest a medieval background. The passionate plea for action places Barker outside the Waste Land of potential energy and in the realm of kinetic energy advocated by Auden's journey poems. But, although Barker cannot indicate with Auden that all past is past, neither can he with the early Eliot be content to record the spiritual decline of his civilization. Barker had, in fact, written that "Mr. Eliot is not a contemporary. He is concerned with problems which have mistakenly entered this century instead of oblivion." [2]

Despite the poem's genuine power, the intellectual core of "Vision of England '38" isn't solid. Exposed to Eliot and Auden, to the greatness of the heroic past and the advantages of a Communist future, Barker isn't, it seems, wholly sure of the solution he advocates. Throughout, he cries for a leader to save England; finally, that hero becomes the working man himself, who has been personified as a mistreated, defenseless female. This association proves to be more than the allegory can digest. Because the conclusion does not arise inevitably from the remainder of the poem, "Vision of England" lacks the organic unity of Barker's most successful verse.

The poem contains, however, other elements which unify it. The vision framework and the element of narrative are used con-

sistently. Allusions to British history and geography provide the
aura of fact appropriate in a protest poem. The irregular quatrains usually contain perfect or half rhyme or one perfect and one
half rhyme ("North," "yard," "starred," "earth"), although sometimes rhyme is sacrificed. The syntax is generally conventional;
organization within sections is associational and, in the broader
scheme, spatial rather than logical. Barker controls progression
largely by using the simple past tense until the final stanza when
he considers the present and the future.

Written in the first person, the poem is filled with vivid, almost
gothic imagery. Barker often moves from the obvious symbol for
an abstraction to a bizarre kind of synecdoche. In context, Shelley
would have been a good allegorical image for reform; but Barker
refers to the poet's skull or to the ghost of Shelley's tear, symbols
one step removed from more conventional allegory, with connotations of their own. The provocative use of color is in the tradition
of Spenser and Keats (the "monster with scales of gold," the
"green girl," the "blue-blooded pen," the North crying "Write it
red").

At the same time that Barker's obsessive use of personification is
obvious, the new realism is sometimes notable:

> But who could whistle or sing in the South
> With its ramshackle witch-barns broken and ruined;
> Where the disused thresher rusts among the lichens,
> And the brood scuttles in the kitchens?

Despite the occasional matter-of-factness, the poem is characteristically expansive; although its uneven and complicated apparatus,
almost unrelieved intensity, and unsure message detract from its
merits, it is one of Barker's major achievements in *Lament and
Triumph.*

IV *Lamentations for Spain*

In 1948 Stephen Spender wrote that "the center of our time was
perhaps the violent, incommunicable death of an innocent victim." [3] Barker's "Elegy on Spain" transforms a picture of such a
victim into a symbol of the martyrdom of Spain. Like the "Vision
of England '38," it is, in a broad sense, an occasional poem; it too
moves from a central experience outward. The nucleus is the

poet's response to the picture of a child killed in an air raid on Barcelona during the Spanish Civil War. Although a protest against Fascism and particularly against the aid Hitler and Mussolini provided Franco and against the timorous nonintervention policy of Great Britain and France, the elegy moves beyond purely political issues to assert that the problem is primarily moral.

At the same time that civil war is a violation of the laws of society—a crime and a murder—it reveals man's endeavor to be the "human brute"; it is a "sin" and the "devil's revel." Barker unites these two concepts to suggest that love—social brotherhood and the creative principle of Christianity—is the only means to ultimate triumph and liberty. Thinking perhaps of the dialectic of Marxism as well as of the cycle of seasonal change and resurrection, he asserts that the death of the child, which "illumines" love, provides the necessary sacrifice that will bring freedom.

In the first publication of the elegy,[4] the picture of a dead boy, pasted on the page opposite the dedication, provides a grim and vivid reality and clarifies imagery which might otherwise seem bizarre. The picture itself is somehow surrealistic: the pose of the dead boy is grotesque. He lies sprawling, with a tag across his breast apparently numbering him among the dead; his long hair seems to be flying out from his head; his mouth is open almost in a gesture of awe or rapture; and one eye is open and staring while the other is ruptured. Barker describes the picture with terrible irony:

> O ecstatic is this head of five-year joy—
> Captured its butterfly rapture on a paper:
> And not the rupture of the right eye may
> Make any less this prettier than a picture.
> O now, my minor moon, dead as meat
> Slapped on a negative plate, I hold
> The crime of the bloody time in my hand.

The juxtaposition of words like ecstatic, joy, rapture, and the colloquial "prettier than a picture" to the flatly realistic "dead as meat/Slapped on a negative plate" creates the bitter irony. The speaker is holding the picture; like John the Baptist, whose head was brought in on a plate, the boy, whose picture is on the film negative, is a sacrifice to wanton brutality. The boy, a minor moon, is the muse of Barker's lament. The child's face in the picture is a round spot of light; the lunar phase suggests blood, and the moon an eternal object responsible for changing tides, as the dead boy comes, metaphorically, to be. The "negative plate" signifies, with "my minor moon," the boy's round face on the photographic film which the speaker holds. The picture frames the poem.

As the "Elegy on Spain" moves outward the boy becomes a hero, a martyr, and a microcosm of the Spanish situation:

> The hero's red rag is laid across his eyes,
> Lies by the Madrid rock and baptizes sand
> Grander than god with the blood of his best, and
> Estramadura is blazing in his fallen hand.

Again we are reminded of Christian martyrdom; for this boy, willfully sacrificed, "baptizes sand" with his blood. The poet mixes microcosm and macrocosm, however; for the boy contains the geographical symbols of Spain's torment. In early 1939, the world of Loyalist sympathizers thought that Madrid was a "rock" that could not be broken; Estramadura was the scene of a bloody battle in Western Spain where peasants fought for the Loyalist cause.

The evil represented by Spain's martyrdom is the destructive element: "Evil lifts a hand and the heads of flowers fall," but it cannot defeat the creative principle which promises recurrence and regeneration—"The spring . . . will not stay under." The boy becomes the monument of the present murderous times and the sacrifice (like the god of fertility rites) which will "water tomorrow with the tears of blood and slaughter." The blossom of hope is nourished by the sacrifice of the boy hero. The poem returns to his unforgettable eyes:

> But now for a moment which shall always be a monument
> Draw like a murder the red rag across those eyes.
> Skies in July not drier than they are,
> Bare of a tear now that pain, like a crystal memorial,
> Is their memorials scattered over the face of Spain.
> Together this hero and the ghost of the Easter Irish,
> Brother and sister, beaten by the fist of the beast,
> Water tomorrow with the tears and blood of slaughter.

Paradoxically, the eyes, no longer able to cry, "water tomorrow."

In Part II the central symbol changes; the poet associates the controlling image of the dying bull with the death of the boy: "Go down, my red bull, proud as a hero." The boy has been transformed into another symbol of gratuitous suffering. The toreador is "the axis pinning Spain through the breast" (and we are suddenly reminded of the butterfly rapture of the boy). The bull does not go down in fair combat, "Beaten by friend, not enemy, betrayed, not beaten. . . ." Combining references to the child and to the bull, Barker concludes Section II with "Draw then the red sky over his eyes. . . .":

> But Spain will not drown,
> For grown to a giantess overnight arises,
> Blazes like morning, Venus on a bleeding sea,
> She, he shall stretch her limbs in liberty.

The third section brings together the image of the boy and the bull in a personification of the center of Spanish resistance, Madrid; the boy's eye and the bull's eye are still upon us, though they are a target for the Fascists:

> Madrid, like a live eye in the Iberian mask,
> Asks help from heaven and receives a bomb:
> Doom makes the night her eyelid, but at dawn
> Drawn is the screen from the bull's-eye capital.

Spain is associated with the "phoenix who leaves ashes/Flashing on the Guernica tree and Guadalajara range." In Guernica, the Republicans had experimented with intensive shellfire; in the 1937 battle of Guadalajara, the Republicans won when rebel tanks failed. Spain's victories suggest her potential for ultimately rising from the ashes of destruction. Good, though "sleeping in the cemeteries of the fallen," is immortal and will, the poet prophesies, return.

Gathering together all of the central symbols and threads of association, the conclusion once more focuses on the individual tragedy:

> So close a moment that long open eye,
> Fly the flag low, and fold over those hands

> Cramped to a gun: gather the child's remains
> Staining the wall and cluttering the drains;
> Troop down the red to the black and the brown;
> Go homeward with tears to water the ground.
> All this builds a bigger plinth for glory,
> Story on story, on which triumph shall be found.

Although the child's obsequies are observed in the plea for treating him with the decencies due the dead, Barker cannot forget that this death is degrading; the child's remains are like so much refuse. The red flag of the hero and martyr and of Communism is to be pulled down by the marching troops of Fascism. The only rites that can be performed for the child are also the only ones that can be observed for Spain. Mourning performs the same function as the martyrdom: tears watering the ground nourish the life that arises from death. A change of heart among Spanish sympathizers is the first step toward new life for Spain.

The concluding metaphysical image seems at first distracting; but, in terms of the associational organization, the architectural reference is effective. The plinth, appropriately a column with this death as its base, is a monument for the boy and the nation. Upon it, rebuilding can begin. Barker has returned to the implications of the end of Part I—the "moment that will always be a monument" and the tear that is "like a crystal memorial." Although the end of the Civil War may leave Spain with only the base of the column, like a tombstone, from it will come final victory. The image contains the basic paradox and asserts the final strength and majesty, the physical reality and solidity of the triumph the poet foresees.

"Elegy on Spain" is one of Barker's most successful political poems because of its overall unity and concentration of emotional power. Its basic synecdoche is revealed in the symbols of the boy, the bull, and Madrid, which Barker successfully interchanges and transforms. It closely approximates the epic form that Barker thought would do more good at the time than any lyric.[5] The poem can be distinguished from most social poetry of the period because of its energy, involvement, and primarily emotional response; controlled and formed by the central symbols, it conveys the horror of the Spanish Civil War and of war itself.

V   *Lamentations for Munich*

The "Seven Munich Elegies" focus fairly consistently on the way in which the evolution of World War II affects the violent man. These poems are not so much about Munich as about the atmosphere of individual despair brought on by the disheartening events of the Munich conference in which England was conciliatory and Hitler demanding—and either war or humiliation for England became inevitable. Despite the grandiose title, the elegies are, therefore, really personal poems.

"Elegy No. 1" establishes the subject matter and attitude, as it moves from public disaster to private significance. Like an Old Testament prophet or like Blake, Barker warns of approaching doom: "In the stage of time the minor moth is small/But prophesies the Fokker with marvellous wings/Mottled with my sun's gold and your sun's blood." Though the Shelleyan moth is small, it flies in wild abandon. The judgment of God is enacted in terms of the present chaos; doom, says the poet, is a huge destructive airplane (God in the guise of man's invention for destruction) whose shadow is the violence of the contemporary scene. Hence the prophet ironically advises a *carpe diem* philosophy:

> Lovers on Sunday in the rear seats of cinemas
> Kiss deep and dark, for is it the last kiss?
> Children sailing on wings in municipal parks
> Swing high, swing high into the reach of the sky,
> Leave, leave the sad star that is about to die.
> Laugh, my comedians, who may not laugh again—Soon, soon,
> Soon Jeremiah Job will be walking among men.

"Elegy No. 1" is an apocalyptic poem, containing many beautiful musical lines; it might have more force, however, if it did not mix the personal crimes of the prophet with those of the world; the persona commits "crimes of rage or rape to ease the ache." The individual's violent reaction to impending doom is ironically the microcosmic manifestation of the sadistic behavior which in the macrocosm so appalls the speaker. The loosely organized poem is perhaps the epitome of irrational prophetic raving.

"Elegy No. 2," written in a more truly elegiac mood, admits ironically and in direct contradiction to "Elegy No. 1" that life goes on. The life it presents is, however, the purposeless sterility of the Waste Land:

> But among the broken glasses and the ticking of the gramaphone,
> From the divan where sex spread an odour of late last night
> Disturbing the collection of fashionable periodicals, yes,
>   Life like Aphrodite rises;
> Scattering tomorrows and shattering yesterdays, rises,
> Rises from the cushions on which my youth has died,
>   Promising impossible prizes
> She dares me to swear that she is the one who will die.

The "autumnal orchards" do not contain the rich harvest; here "apples like dried worms dangle from branches" and the "barking tractor has/Shorn off the glory of auburn July." The poet's mood shifts from optimism to pessimism: "Thus alternate day and dark."

The third elegy treats the speaker's wandering search for integration of the dual aspects of his personality; his life is admittedly that of a monster, half bull, half man ("My minotaur life lost in London's mazes"). While looking for fulfillment, he torments himself: "When I like Caesar lie bleeding/Who bares the Brutus knife if not I?" Tormentor and tormented, demagogue and misguided leader, idealist and assassin, he is a self-divided creature. The aspiring idealist is an ascetic who hates the body and wishes to escape it, although he admits the attractions of the world (with an echo of Dylan Thomas' "It is the sinner's dust-tongued bell"): "Dust on the tongue is sweet." The things of sense are "brilliant ephemerae . . . gay chaos . . . a revelation of momentary wonder and life" difficult to relinquish. Although the persona, echoing "Ash Wednesday," does not wish to "turn again," his senses tell him to turn toward life:

> The bells of the bluebell peal and appeal.
> So on the tongues of things I'm torn—
> Do I dare forward as I cannot backward?
> —It is all part of a paradise of pain.
> I shall not turn again.

Language reminiscent of Eliot is turned to the purposes of nihilism and to the conflict between Eros and the death wish.

In "Elegy No. 5" everything is seen to be in conflict; things of positive value contain their opposites:

> Scope of the star is space where aeronauts die;
> Range of the wave is deep where the ships go down;
> Those who climb high hit heads against the sky;
> Deep enough in reflection all things drown.
>   The double function of all faces
> Kisses as it kisses its lover to a liar:
> I shall not tread those marvellous surfaces,
>   For ice is fire.

Life seems to have no meaning and little value: "What is it all but a Woolworth welter of things . . . ?" Achievement is never certain; the only thing certain is death. This mood of disillusionment continues in "Elegy 6" where the persona forsakes looking to the infinite for guidance. Although he recalls "my one-time ecstasies from Doldrums," the dolphins of delight are lost since he has brought his "hulk to the home of Europe." The poet juxtaposes despairing nihilism to an ambivalent faith in living dangerously: "Passion is suicide by which life is proven:/I am the dead, the only happy one."

Although most of the Munich Elegies express personal loss and nihilism, the final elegy moves to the broader social scene. Bringing together the images of gnashing gears and crushing wheels used to begin the elegies, it embodies the idea of Time and Becoming as a creative-destructive continuum which uses the individual in a Newtonian universe where he is ground out of the flux like oil:

> Nevertheless when the hands cross at midnight and noon
> O golden oil spills and from the wheels' mesh
> Time produces its patterns of fate on the flesh,
> And I shall fall out like golden oil from the clash.
> Not then, though the axle cracks or the wheels veer
>   To miss my skull—
> I feel the jewelled rims riding up my skin
> To leave me drawn and quartered in the rear.

The brilliant clock image perhaps owes something to the Brahmin concept of Maya, the wheel of life out of which the individual

sometimes falls. The mixed metaphor of the final line detracts
from the otherwise dazzling imagery to suggest the individual's
ignominious position in life.

The final stanza captures in bold, controlled music the dominant mood of the late 1930's:

> Therefore be generous among friends with kisses,
> Hold parties of domestic dance and song—
>   O make the doomed roof ring:
> Join me in celebrating the occasions of bliss
> That turned a condemned home to a ballroom
> Ballooned with laughter and ribboned with love.
>   The lights will go out soon
> And the sound of the mooning bomber drone above.

In a sense, the "Munich Elegies" are retrogressive; for they display a personal, sometimes unhealthy reaction to the unhappy
times; sometimes the brilliant and chaotically associated imagery
is not worth the effort it takes to comprehend the despair that
informs it. Other political poems written by Barker in the early
1940's are more persistently concerned with the social scene.

VI   *The Prophet as Political Analyst*

The "New Poems" section of *Selected Poems* (1941) examines
the sociopolitical world. Barker's stay in the United States inspired his "American Odes," three of his least successful diagnostic
poems. Attempting to fill a vast canvas with the obvious, they fail
to achieve positive organic unity. The "First American Ode" is
typical—a lesson in historical name-dropping, a Whitmanesque
catalogue whose details have no focal point. The extensive,
sprawling, somewhat ranting poem contains little that Barker
didn't say better in "Vision of England '38" or "Elegy on Spain,"
except that the villain has changed. The speaker hopes that tomorrow will not "descend/Through narrowing spirals of avarice
and chicanery/Till the seventh son of Rockefeller, in the
centre,/Stands like Imperator."

"Requiem Anthem for the Austrian Constitution," is an occasional
poem under whose verbal paraphernalia any genuine feeling
for the collapse of Austria is crushed. The imagery for celebrating
this public disaster is strangely personal. Like the "Kings with
diamonds in their eyes" (presumably the Hapsburgs) the poet

seems to be "Mopping [*sic*] and mowing among private shadows."
As in the "American Odes," the analysis is oversimplified and the
solution too pat. The requiem for the *Anschluss* will, the poet promises,"drum on the time their bloody assassination"; the poem
literally then drums on the theme of time with "Time is with them
. . . Time is with them . . . Time is more with them." The political situation seems simply another occasion for lamenting the present and for hoping for a future triumph. The poet's indignation
is so generalized and so detached from the real circumstances that
he cannot find an appropriate framework for composition. The
Austrian "Requiem" does not convey the solemnity and sincerity
of a mass for the repose of souls of the dead.

Barker is more successful when his strategy involves the use of a
central symbol or some device beyond mere chronological order
for creating unity. "The Neo-Geordies," although even more narrowly topical than the "Austrian Requiem," is a better political
poem. Like "Geordie," the popular ballad from which it derives its
name, Barker's is a historical ballad. It concerns the events leading
up to World War II and modern heroes who might stir the popular imagination. Geordie was a nobleman captured for poaching,
a political charge that merited severe punishment at the time of
the ballad's origination. In some versions Geordie is saved by his
lady's pleading; in others, despite her supplications, he is hanged
in chains of gold that signify his noble birth.

Barker's ballad protests against the injustices done to those who
opposed Hitler and Mussolini, those like Niemoller, Benes, and
Haile Selassie who were literally or figuratively imprisoned and
punished for their opposition (ineffective or tardy) to unethical
political and military tactics. Each of the "Neo-Geordies" is envi-
sioned as a gallant but frustrated friend of freedom. The elegant
chains in which Geordie was hanged become a symbol of the ineffectual support of lost causes. Barker, the political analyst, reveals a pattern in the behavior of noble leaders whose political
careers ended in humiliation or who could not act in the face of
aggression.

"The Ballad of the Three Dead and the Three Living" is more
successful than "The Neo-Geordies" because not so topical. It di-
agnoses modern culture in a simple, direct narrative with allegorical implications. Although the visual imagery is surrealistic, it successfully conveys meaning. Three men in a limousine "Travelling

westward" toward death "Passed three men" just like themselves
"Travelling upward." The vertical travelers represent the deaths
toward which the horizontal travelers move, and the upward
movement outside of time represents Being, the movement "westward" Becoming. The men in the flux are too interested in their
sensual pleasures to pay attention to death which is always imminent. Their pleasures are epitomized in three sins—lust ("they
handled their queans"), gluttony ("They thought of the white
wines/And the sweetmeats"), and avarice ("They looked at their
phosphorescent watches and flashed/Gold rings"). These are
among the seven capital sins punishable by spiritual death; but
the proud capitalists are ironically already spiritually dead and
will not heed the warning of their approaching end.

VII   *The Struggle Within*

Barker's vision of life as tension between dualities is implicit in
"The Ballad of the Three Living and the Three Dead"; in the
"Holy Poems," the struggle is accepted as primarily religious and
as specifically Christian. As a unit, these four poems record the
conflict with doubt. The speaker wrests hope for individual immortality from a despairing dualism in which "Satan is triumphant at one side of me" (I). To accept faith and love, he transcends his horror of the world tragedy that he augurs, despite
man's paradoxical condition (II). "Anticipating trumpets" of
apocalyptic revelation and judgment, the "truant" from "the
tomb" is warned of approaching doom by God's messenger and
warrior angel Gabriel (III). As the mystical prophet of revelation, the speaker finally sees life as the real martyrdom in which
man suffers for the hope of eventual release and awaits the final
meeting with God in the terrible glory of death (IV). Like the
Old Testament prophet, he arraigns mankind's destructive bestiality, "Our smile . . . bright with tiger," which dooms "us down"
before God makes his entrance to end the insignificant single life.

The "Holy Poems" are full of grim prognostications of holocaust
and of wild hopes that physical dissolution will mean spiritual
release. When Nimrod, the mighty biblical hunter and militarist,
warns the poet "to keep from blood" and to "Turn back the mad
tides of the time with Truth," the central dichotomy is clear (I).
Passion ("Mad blood") is contrasted to the absolute value of
Truth which "can move the seas behind the breast." The poet-

prophet insists that "a wink of wonder" should move man more than his tendencies toward violence. Passionately aware of both his strength and his weakness, the Romantic sees in himself the absolute antitheses, identifying with the protagonist and the antagonist of the moral drama:

> Siamese monster of Christ and the Devil
> I coil my sins in ecstasy around me:
> Bound in the centre, martyred to my evil,
> Burning with yearning the God I in me
> Melts like a candle of tears to see
> Satan triumphant at one side of me.
> O my left side where Hell inhabits me!

The microcosm is the universe with its own cosmology of incompatible heaven and hell. Although the promethean prototype wants to be his own deliverer, the Perseus of a "world within a world" who releases the soul, he is aware of his unwarrantable boldness: "Who, what am I to drop down from the sky/Shaking a word's sword . . . ?"

Even the violent pagan of history, dead and no more significant than a host for a parasite, knows more of the answers than the poet does:

> Tamburlaine makes a magnificent mushroom
> . . . .
> But though no more than a spot of rot, he knows
> More than I know, the holy name and home.

The speaker's pagan gods are not very reassuring either: Narcissus suggests that death is final loss, for there would be no more self to love; and Venus, though "my sweet star," is, in her beauty and ascendancy, a contrast to the poet's own uncertainty: "I not so fine and not so vivid whistle/Of heaven. . . ." Christ and Satan are only two of the opposites at war; the central contrast is expressed, on the one hand, with allusions to Nimrod, Satan, Tamburlaine, and Narcissus, and, on the other, with references to Truth, Christ, Perseus, and Venus.

The whistling in the dark of the first of the "Holy Poems" becomes victory in the second, but only after the persona has submitted himself, for the moment, to the blind acceptance of faith, despite the evidences of a cruel God and a miserable world. Individual tragedy is related to a dynamic universe whose history is cyclical, "a world that never rests,/Whistling and swinging down the recurring West." The poet-prophet refers to war in Europe "With blood-prognosticating eyes" and asserts that only Love (apparently simultaneously brotherly love and divine intervention) can "halt the funeral" brought on by the Satanic pride of Europe's "Imperial Eagles." Obsessed with discovering a way to affirm the tragedy of life, the Romantic does not relinquish his hope of heaven, "the high world I seek," although he rides "instead the angel-infested wave,/Attesting that a mystery crowns our lives/With the smile of God's blood-flecked jaws." And, when the world destroys itself, the yea-sayer, who can praise or love in spite of the horror, shall have earned his immortality: he can assert a triumphant immortality: "Then with a shout I shall leap out/ Among the loud angel-infested crowd;/And, whistling, show the glory of my shroud."

But the naïve poet, "chasing the rainbow," is reminded in "Holy Poem III" to prepare for approaching doom. Gabriel advises him to forsake self-love, "Lying and gazing at the distorted form/Below me in the water." Aware that the greatest temptation for the Romantic sensibility is self-adulation, Barker had already asserted in the first of these poems that narcissism means spiritual death. In the second poem the self-confident persona displayed his courage to accept life and to earn his immortality; now he expects the consequences. Like the biblical prophet, he awaits the Apocalypse, "to see God in his thunder," an avenging cowboy (like Thomas' "Two-gunned Gabriel") or a fire-bowelled celestial railroad (like Hawthorne's). Like a sinner at a revival meeting, in "terror of tomorrow," he cringes before the calls of judgment. Death is no longer the haven it formerly seemed, but the hell-fire and brimstone that the "evangelists singing in the streets/Tell me of." The "grave/Is now myth haunted by God" who will "smother me like a father/Mothering the son still hanging in his thigh."

The final image is perhaps unsatisfactory. In trying to convey the contradictory relationship of man to God, who is both creator and destroyer, Barker uses bizarre paradox. The idea of a father, as it were, nourishing the potential child he harbors in his thigh by "smothering" while mothering almost suggests an ugly onanism. The ambiguity is overwrought, but it indicates the distrust of Godhead which becomes a major theme in later poetry.

In the fourth Holy Poem alienation from God is the subject. The speaker is, in his heart, an exiled Saint (Saint John of Patmos), tempted by "Black Michaels and gold Satans" to forsake his "marvellous mountains" of revelation. Because appearances are so deceiving—Michael, God's conquering angel, looks evil; and Satan, God's enemy, golden and good—he wants to remain in the mystic's retreat where love is the primal element, "Spinoza's face hanging from every tree/Murmuring love of all our kith and kind." The visionary longs for his "apocalyptic home."

Whether he is "Sebastian's brother," martyred in the cause of Christianity, or Haman, the enemy of God's chosen people hanged on gallows he had prepared for a Jew—he would be happy in death; whether he is the martyr or the tormentor caught in his own plot, death is preferable to life. "There is no martyrdom worse than a life," which cannot, if one aspires to be a Christian, be escaped by suicide or by literal or spiritual castration: "I cannot cut my body to Saint Peter's key/Or, nipping off the hip-rose with a knife/Make me archangel. . . ." Nor can he escape life's torment by betraying Christ, like a Judas; for no one is interested in buying "my master" who is only an effigy of the real Jesus, a "plaster Jesus" who turns out to be himself. The persona cannot get himself out of the center of vision to let Christ in: the make-believe Jesus is "Crossed on my pain and crucified in my eye."

Finally the speaker (Stanza 3) identifies himself with all mankind, condemned for brutality:

> The monarch who wears a shrieking crown
> Is us. All whipping tongues and words
> Flash at our head and doom us down:
> The sex of our cherubim is swords.
>
> . . . .
> Our smile is bright with tiger . . .

The violent contrast of cherubs and swords, of smile and tiger, indicates man's underlying ambivalence; he is caught up and forced into action in the dynamic process of life: "the days/Turn us like dogs in their drums." The apocalyptic poet finally envisions God coming among men to release them from life's pain:

> Then comes
> Spinning and shining among us like wheels,
> Throwing off visions to lead us home,
> God—snatches me up in finger and thumb,
> Douses me like a glimmer. And I see
> Cruel to be kind to all his kind is he.

The three stanzas of "Holy Poem IV" are organized by the correspondence between the great world of John's Revelation and
the little world of the poet-prophet. Although the final paradox,
borrowed from Shakespeare, conveys the basically Christian idea
of destroying to save, the underlying attitude suggests the Gnosticism which repeatedly tempts Barker. Despair weights the case
for evil. All matter seems to be bestial and the claims of the body
wrong. The speaker both resents and respects the creator who
treats man like a pet (a dog) or an instrument to beat (a drum)
or a candle to be snuffed by the saving destroyer and destroying
saviour.

The struggle between angel and devil, spirit and flesh, is also
manifest in poems about love and procreation. "Love Poem I" in
the "New Poems" section of *Selected Poems* asserts the disillusioned attitude toward love, which Barker associates more and
more with original sin. The poem is primarily about the creative
principle, "the cyclic passion of compulsive birth," but it reveals
the Gnostic aversion to sex coupled, at the same time, with masculine desire: "So to my bed I lead a Sheba of Harpies/Who tears
me down to the quicks of sense/And shows me Adam coiling in
my hips." He cannot, however, resist praising the prolific female
who suffers in childbirth:

> when you bleed,
> The gush of love will garb the sinning human
> In O magnanimous garments of all sympathy
> And so, at last, messiah be a woman.

The imagery is dominantly natural and physiological: "the spawn
. . . the bag of birth . . . the singing seed . . . her x of breed
. . . Cupid drops from her hips . . . the womb . . . abdomen
. . . your labours." Juxtaposed are images of fertility in nature:
"the green tree, green and gold, harvest,/O lakes that sigh to meet
the sea, all our origins rise from these: simple sea . . . river,

water. . . ." The little world of woman corresponds to the prolific universe.

Although the first love poem asserts the relationship of the erotic impulse to morality, "Love Poem 2," submitting love to the analysis of science, concludes ambivalently that it is largely a biological urge which is, however, controverted by the moment of fulfillment. The conflicting feelings are clear in "X is my cross and love is my resurrection":

> Who was a sleeping Venus is a demon who
> Clutches my vision down from ever green heaven
> Strips O the seven marvellous veils from even
> You and reveals the agnostic genetic engine.

Despite intimations of Freudian sexual determinism, the male in the sex act is a kind of God who holds "you, golden, [in] my Jehovah hand," and resurrects and is resurrected through love.

A "new poem" about unfulfilled love, "No Other Tiger Walked that Way that Night" is a sensual, Surrealist painting of the Romantic agony,[6] developed and embellished through a central symbol, the tigress who represents a forsaken woman. The tiger, something like Blake's, is a symbol for creative energy and passion; for Barker, creative energy is intensely physical and, in fact, sexual. The tiger is the male lover epitomized. The woman's anguish is conveyed through the terrible tension set up between desire and frustration, between the tigress' determination to cherish the memory of her mate and her real need for another, although "no other tiger walked that way." The sheer sensuality of the language saves the poem from descending to bathos.

The imagery suggests the all-consuming power of frustrated passion which involves the woman's whole anatomy: she offers herself to her lover, hand, head and heart. Surrealistic images distort visual reality to connote her irrational desire: "She tied her hand with promises to the gate/She gave her head in red on a golden plate,/She hung her heart out in a begging arm." In short, she shamelessly humiliated herself: "She wound her bowels out around a tree/She shed astrologies of tears; she bled/Til the seas choked with love unsatisfied." It seems she had reason to feel forsaken, for "The sabre-toothed baby wrestled in its lair/Among her memories of an amorous May,"and "she opened her future like a gate," but "No other tiger ever entered there." The lair is the womb, probably opening the future for the birth of a child.

Barker does not sentimentalize her; on the contrary he presents her excesses—she does everything in "superlatives." The poem is about a kind of person, excessive but real, Dionysian or Lawrention, a kind of Molly Bloom with a capacity for idealizing sexual love. The obvious sensuality and seeming decadence of the subject matter are aspects of his work which Barker currently repudiates.

VIII   *Characteristics of the Middle Poems*

A poem more characteristic of Barker's middle phase is "Summer Idyll" which also appeared in the "New Poems" section of *Selected Poems*. It combines sensuous imagery with a keen objective focus, while moving from a general description of summer's fecundity to a description of what the poor do in the hot, close weather. Tension is created in the contrast between the summer richness and "poverty pulling down/The tautened boughs." The poor might be better off dead: the heat, "pressure upon their lives like deep/Seas, becomes, insufferable." They bathe, chase rabbits, idle "Strewn/Over the parks like soiled paper like summer/Insects," wander in gardens "seduced by the pure Beauty, like drowned men floating in bright coral," or go "up the river in boats" and "in the water shadows/Trail a hand, which need not find a bank,/Face downward, like bad fruit." The similes imply the poet's reaction to the scene: the people are drowning; they are blemishes on the landscape, a kind of refuse, insignificant, numerous and almost subhuman. The overpowering richness puts a terrible pressure upon "their spare bodies" and spirits; and the irony of the title becomes apparent. The poem succeeds within its limited scope; the surprisingly rich visual imagery communicates the smothering opulence of the season; and summer in the city is seen and felt.

"No Other Tiger Walked that Way that Night" and "Summer Idyll" perhaps represent the two extremes in the poetry Barker published between 1939 and 1941. The one is sensual, exotic, Surrealistic; the other, sensuous, direct, almost Naturalistic. Although most of those middle poems derive from the real, political world, Barker's approach is dominantly subjective. The poet-prophet transmits the world scene, through the prism of his personality, onto a canvas huge and alive with symbols. At their best, these poems—the first of his middle period—illustrate the dynamic philosophy of resolving opposites through the agency of the imagination. The idea is not just a truism; it becomes Barker's method of facing the world, or of absorbing it and transforming it into symbols which themselves almost invariably stand for conflicting ideas. The approach is not so irrational as it may seem in some of the less successful poems. And Barker, like any serious poet, deserves to be judged for his best, not his worst work.

The moral order in the intense drama that the poet-prophet lives is the one we find in Shelley's *Prometheus,* in Byron's *Cain,* in Blake's prophecies, and in the late Yeats. It is no accident that in this period Barker comes to see in Yeats "the lunar emperor whom Time could not break," the "sense of action," and the duality of "Saints on mountains or animals in the ground" [7] that constitutes his own outlook. *Lament and Triumph* and "New Poems" reflect the desire to fuse earth and heaven, finite and infinite, real and ideal, microcosm and macrocosm. Even the wildest auguries lament the organized chaos of modern life where man has forgotten the imminence of the infinite.

Barker's new awareness of mankind leads to his political vision, which, in turn, provokes his concern for the moral and cosmic implications of world crisis. He becomes preoccupied with a sense of mission as the herald of impending doom and with analyzing the struggle within the individual between the divine and the demonic. Although all of the poems reveal a new respect for fact, as tension regarding man's sad state mounts, wild juxtapositions of contradictory symbols, arch comparisons, highly sensuous and allusive language convey explosive feeling. Parallels to the Old Testament or Revelations are clear; the prophetic poetry foreshadows the subject matter of writers of the New Apocalypse—"the crisis of Spirit." [8] In revealing the meaning of the hell and death of the modern world, Barker asserts the value of their opposites and makes poetry of the dualities. At their worst, the middle poems are full of empty rhetoric; at their best, they represent the artistic reconciliation of interpenetrating opposites and a prophecy of better things to come.

CHAPTER 5

Eros in Dogma:
Why Are All Things So?

THE line of development that emerged in *Lament and Tri-umph* and "New Poems" reaches its apex in *Eros in Dogma* (1944). It questions "all things/That suffer and do not die" (49). Like Nietzsche's madman, Barker cries, "Whither is God?" Like Byron's Cain, he asks "Why are all things so?" [1] His acute response to the political scene necessitated bringing together private and public experience.

The "Pacific Sonnets," which form the first section of *Eros in Dogma,* display the interaction of the poet and his environment as well as his recollection in enforced tranquillity of things past. Although first published in the "New Poems" section of *Selected Poems,* they form a transition between the style and subjects of the poetry treated in Chapter 4 and the manner and matter of *Eros in Dogma.* Although undoubtedly written before the "American Odes," the sonnets rightly assume the initial position in the 1944 volume; for they form the background for the "Sacred and Secular Elegies" and reveal refinements of style characteristic of the whole book.

I *Poet in Exile*

As records of Barker's six months in Japan as a professor of English literature at the University of Sendai, they reveal the poet in a Pacific exile. Barker writes of his reaction to the war fermenting in Europe, to the self-imposed loneliness, to the Japanese culture, and to the problem of individual suffering and death. After he came to the United States, his responses were published in essays in *The New Republic* and *The New Yorker* as "Notes from the Largest Imaginary Empire" and "The Improbable Empire." The "inscrutability" and "whimsicality" of Japan, its placidity and formalities, exasperated Barker. He thought the "Japanese intelligence . . . extremely prone to the pursuit of hares or conquests of patents." [2] The essentially dynamic Romantic despised the "long time lag . . . which intervenes between the question and the answer or the proposition and its execution." [3] The sojourn may have tempered certain of his early views, for Japanese "moongazing" and "that final gesture of the dissatisfied romantic, a theatrical death," seem at the time despicable to him. [4]

The Pacific Sonnets can be read almost as a single poem—a theme and variations, a genus and differentiae: the genus is the title, which is also the locus of the poems—"Pacific" sonnets. The title locates the poems geographically; indicates the artist's physical situation, caught in an inactive state away from and unable to do anything about the things really important to him; and implies the disciplined restraint of the verse form Barker had chosen. Finally, the title is an ironic reference to the tension that informs the poems.

The opening sonnet establishes the tone and themes:

> Between the wall of China and my heart
> O exile is. Remembering the tremendous
> Autumnals of nations threatening to end us all,
> I speak of the things nearest to my heart.
> These space cannot alienate, or time part
> From me: O is it really an end of them
> The flowering moments that a poem blends
> To Babylonian wreaths around my heart?

The war prophesied is both tragic and ironic: "O how the eighteen year olds in stupefaction/Go stepping pretty into an imperial monument!" (II). The memory of the boy killed in Barcelona comes alive in new guises, in a reaction brought about by very specific stimuli from the war in Europe (VI, XI); Barker cannot forget the "Messerschmitt's domination" (V), Europe shrieking in her death throes(V), and the fall of Poland(X). At one point the persona, despite "the postures and disguises/Of loss and defeat and even Europe" (XII), cries out with sentiment parallel to Auden's famous conclusion to "September, 1939": "O it is love we must have"(XIV). But the preponderant evidence is that we cannot escape our tragic human condition(XIII, XV), that we can therefore learn how "to suffer, not how to die"(XVI), despite the irony of belonging to a scapegoat generation that shoulders blame for conditions it did not cause.

When Barker turns to his intense reaction to individual death in a senseless war, his bitterness leads to direct, biting statement:

> And now there is nothing left to celebrate
> But the individual death in a ditch or a plane
>
> . . . .
>
> This is the only dignity left, the single
> Death without purpose and without understanding
> Like birds boys drop with catapults. Not comprehending
> Denudes us of the personal aim and angle,
> And so we are perfect sacrifice to nothing.

Barker celebrates this "death for which no one is ready" (VIII) in his much anthologized "Three Memorial Sonnets for two young seamen lost overboard in a storm in Mid Pacific, January, 1940" (VII, VIII, IX). The first begins in an acutely apprehended image of a real event. It concerns, however, the emotional response of the speaker whose attention is riveted to the horrifying scene:

> The seagull spreadeagled splayed on the wind
> Span backwards shrieking, belly facing upward,
> Fled backward with a gimlet in its heart
> To see the two youths swimming hand in hand
> Through green eternity.

The opening image, with its compelling visual and auditory impact, establishes the scene; the action of the bird parallels, at the same time, the fall of the two sailors, swept backward into the water, and the feelings of the stunned spectator, pierced with dread at the moment of their fall. The violent imagery of the octave is appropriate and essential for picturing the event, for suggesting the stormy sea and the terror of the seamen, and for presenting the speaker's tumultuous feelings. Barker personifies the sea first as a giant with jaws that will swallow the men and then suggests a *femme fatale* whose waves are flouncing skirts. The men themselves look, ironically, like lovers. The speaker, unable to move or to think rationally, is overwhelmed by "pity's peace"—the seeming calm of one dumbstruck by "vague horror."

The octave centers implicitly on the speaker's visual and emotional response; the sestet discloses the point of view. Even the disparate similes of the "hand flapping like a flag . . ./And another like a dolphin with a child supporting him" are images inspired in the observer by the ineffectual gestures of the floundering seamen. He wonders whether he "Was . . . the shape of Jesus" (the sailors' hope for mercy or the form of their judgment) to the drowning men in whose rolling eyes he interprets looks of supplication. The automatic gesture of terror-stricken appeal is grimly communicated by "the eyeballs swivelled." The turbulent sea, the sailors, and the state of the speaker are simultaneously suggested by the startling images.

The second sonnet centers on the violent storm and the speaker's feeling of entrapment as he empathizes with the sailors. Because this sonnet does not concern his immediate reaction, it is properly more consistent than the first. Controlled by a series of associations, all of which use the relationship of containers to things contained, it formulates the speaker's fear, no longer "vague horror," but now defined as fear of enclosure—his own fear of drowning. The poem itself comes from inside the storm ("From thorax of storms . . . like the silence/Round which cyclones rage"); so real is the empathy that the speaker tastes the "sea swilling" in his bowels; sitting in the "swing of waves," aware of his insignificance before the elemental fury, he is "Like a face in a bubble"; and the sailors are in the "guts" of the "greedy bitch." The human factors are caught or swallowed by the sea. Deriving from the central pattern, the final image of man's paltry place before the great devourer comes through forcefully: the sea tosses the husk of man, his body, into her mouth, as if it were so much refuse to be eaten by the piggish female death.

The third sonnet focuses on the sailors. After the first treats the impact on the speaker of the sailors' fall and the second his identification with their doom, the third completes the trilogy with a relatively detached view. The octave describes the spectator's vivid impression of the actual drowning; the sestet remarks with irony and objectivity that quick death without tears is at least a victory over the hollow conventional observances usually associated with death. The "useless tear that did not fall/ . . . was the prize"; the pitiless speed of the drowning marks it as unusual, an event deviating from what men know about dying. The fact that they had no time for tears is the only substitute the seamen are granted for the customary rites marked by "The flowers, the gifts,

the crystal sepulchre . . . /The perfect and nonexistent obsequies." The catalogue, in apposition to "the prize" (the tear not
shed, which paradoxically provides a memorial for the dead
men), refers to the usual tokens of rites of passage, which, because
they are performed with ceremonial correctness, are perfect; but,
because they are sanctimonious and have little to do with the actual fact of death, they are not really obsequies. Wilfred Owen's
"Anthem for Doomed Youth" and Dylan Thomas' "A Refusal to
Mourn . . ." disclose similar attitudes toward the reality of violent death.

Technically, the three sonnets of Barker reflect the influence of Hopkins. The first lines, "The seagull, spreadeagled,
splayed . . . ," adapt Hopkins' alliterative technique to imply the
sense of helplessness and the remorseless movement of nature toward death. Carefully wrought consonance, such as the shrieking
"s' s" that sweep through the first sonnet like a great wind, contrib-
utes to a music contrived to transmit urgency and shock. The in-
versions and daring use of the effusive "O," as well as the sprung
rhythm of "Then, then the shock, the last gasp of breath," appropriately express internal stress. The metrical roughness within an
otherwise tightly controlled form enforces the central tension between the inescapable fact of death and the equally inescapable
fact that witnessing it inspires an awful empathy. Death is as inevitable to man as fourteen lines are to the sonnet, but a man
experiencing death vicariously cannot accept it in unquavering
iambic pentameter or in perfect sonnet rhyme scheme. The off
rhyme ("wind-hand"; "waves-heaves"; "silence-balance"; "randy-
ready"; "God-load") captures the dissonant quality of the experience.

The three poems study reactions to violent death by water;.
they become movements of one poem whose dialectical imagery
completes the picture of and response to drowning. The many
indications of setting (the seagull, green water, cabins, bulwark,
stern) merge with the archetypal sea imagery of the devouring
mother (clearest in Sonnet VII, but suggested by jaws and skirts.
in VIII and by the "green arms around them" in IX) in juxtaposition to suggestions of a conventional Christian reaction which is.
finally rejected as irrelevant. The sestet of VIII reminds us that
the elemental amoral female is "formidable as God"; the eternity

she brings is green because it means drowning forever in her waters. The octave of IX reiterates the entreaty first suggested in
VII; but, when the seamen looked up at the noon sun, they knew
with terrible certainty that they would die. Similes indicate that,
for the sailors, it was Doomsday, "loud as thunder/As white as
angels and as broad as God." The sestet concludes that, despite
their seeming appeal for supernatural aid in the first poem, the
only miracle is that they did not suffer more. Although the sea is
like God and death like His judgment, the spectator accepts with
secular courage the fact of inexorable and ultimate death.

Even the final ironic approval of the way in which the sailors
died is appropriate to the emotional development of the trilogy
from the shock of the first, to the shudder of the second, to the
grim serenity of the third poem. Barker skillfully equates the dramatic pattern to the course of the tempest and the tempestuous
action. All of the elements work together to transmit the initial
impact of the event, the speaker's subsequent horror, and his final
resignation. The sequence is an eloquently inscribed memorial for
the lost seamen.

II   *Elegies in Search of a Dogma*

When "Pacific Sonnets" were first published, the last in the
series was the sonnet placed at the conclusion of *Eros in Dogma,*
"To any Member of My Generation." Malcolm Cowley wrote of
this that Barker has "a gift for making final statements. Nobody
else has expressed so well the feeling of guilt that oppresses this
generation as Barker has done in the last six lines of his 'Pacific
Sonnets' ":

> Whenever we kissed we cocked the future's rifles
> And from our wild-oat words, like dragon's teeth,
> Death under foot now arises: when we were gay
> Dancing together in what we hoped was life,
> Who was it in our arms but the whores of death
> Whom we have found in our beds today, today? [5]

Feelings of guilt and disillusionment are intensified in the "Sacred
and Secular Elegies" which are the poetic statement of the esthetic
Barker announced in his 1940 essay, "Therefore All Poems are

Elegies." Haunted by a dark view of the world, the Romantic pounds upon the gates of the absolute, suffering at the mercy of his senses and over the cosmology of existence.

At first glance, even the title of this group reflects the conflict between two worlds, the secular and the sacred. The poems do not, however, reveal a sharp dichotomy: the "Secular Elegies" lament a Godless world while seeking a secular mythology, and the "Sacred Elegies" lament a world where man is estranged from tradition and God. In relation to the subject matter, the common meaning of "sacred" is ironic; although "holy" is hardly the right description for the elegies, the less common meaning of "sacred" —baleful or accursed—reflects the dominant feeling of the poems.

The first two "Secular Elegies" are unquestionably political. "Elegy I" presents an attitude typifying public and intellectual opinion at the time of World War II. Barker criticizes "My pig-faced kingdom with tongues of wrong/And an historical gait of trial and error." He asks for decisive action: "Now answer history with a marvellous golden Yes/As she steps up asking all future questions." He advises England as to what should constitute the positive answer. Comparing Britain's war tactics to those of a bird, the poem asserts that the bird, "after the reverses,/Perches whistling on the shattered axles proudly." It warns of the "catch-penny Caesars"—the Fascist dictators—and supplicates heroes to be wary for "when you close an eye your life is over." Nonetheless, the English position will not be nearly so bad as that of its enemies who fight for a cause with bad conscience:

> They will not ever really die, but continually
> Thrash on the hotbed of their animus:
> Not one of them shall die hopefully and finally
> For them the grave will also be full of us.

"Elegy II" alleges the inevitability of political awareness and action in times such as these. The lessons of history cannot be overlooked now; all things are transformed by the political situation. Barker attributes the symbol-making power to all men. The "cyclist" who "formerly . . . saw birds in bushes" now sees "Cromwell," a symbol of former leadership coming from the citizenry when the royal government failed (so the Roundheads thought) in its responsibility. The past admonishes the present. Bentham's truism that "What makes the people happiest is best" is juxtaposed to an image which indicates the discrepancy between truth and reality: "The fish in its undersea caves and the bird in its nest/Know that the shark and cuckoo never rest." The images of animal predators provide a warning and a transition to prophecy. Lessons of history must be supplemented by those of biology: even lowly creatures instinctively know what Great Britain seems to ignore—the lesson of survival.

Barker envisions a series of retreats from Fascism, even though "The hakencreutz accumulates but never masters." Some read their dooms in their palms; others, says the poet in ironic reply to the brotherhood Auden and he himself had formerly espoused, "Who came kissing and bringing olives,/Had a change of heart and are dead now." Barker is no doubt thinking of the "Neo-Geordies" who approached Hitler and Mussolini peacefully and were coerced into capitulation. In trying to understand the times, Barker realizes that chance might have made any of us into the doubters, the dead, or even the destroyers. He alludes to Pascal— " 'My friend, my friend, you were born out on the other side' "—to imply that people suffer simply because they are born in particular locations. Pascal's notion that justice is relative—that justice on one side of the river is injustice on the other—[6] leads to the assertion of man's freedom and responsibility. From Barker's argument it follows that we are all at fault for the miseries of war. No matter on which side we were born, we are guilty: "O the demented/ Alexander, who, eternally discontented,/Desires more, is us. Finally we die of pride."

Whereas "Secular Elegy II" is about the world, "Elegy III" ("Satan is on your tongue . . .") concerns the devil, the flesh, and the world, in that order. It indicts the individual, lovers, and mankind. The poet, "Sweet singer," succumbs to the Satanic temptations of material gain and praise or fame—the "income and the encomium"—but angels, in contrast, "rhapsodise for and from their faith." The modern poet, who has traded divine inspiration for secular values, falls short of an exalted concept of the poet.

However, the self-sufficient romantic tells us that we can control "the principle of evil" with "the whip of the will." Free will is not, however, easily reconciled with foreordination; Barker asks the overwhelming question:

Thus if the crux and judgment never is
Left to our own to do with as we will
But the decision, like a master key, lies
Wholly in the higher hands that hold all—
How can we be as innocent as this?

If a good God controls our destinies, how can He let us be so
naïve as to be seduced by evil or to believe the myth Lucifer uses
to seduce the Adamic Orpheus? Barker believes, and he alludes to
Nietzsche (and perhaps at the same time to Yeats) as an authority, that the most profound truths are the greatest enigmas:
"Everything that is profound loves the mask." Thus free will may
masquerade as foreordination and foreordination as free will. But
most important, in modern society, the damning sin masquerades
as "a necessary satisfaction." Biology and psychology have led us
to believe that the satisfaction of the sexual urge is necessary. The
sin of sex wears the mask of love, which is bestiality in disguise.
When lovers embrace, "the beast is bare:/It is not Love but
double damnation there." Barker poses a Gnostic attitude against
the views of modern psychology and romantic love.

Now the myth by which Orpheus is seduced is clear: Satan
wins Orpheus to the side of evil by convincing him that love is a
value worth risking hell for and that dead love (Eurydice in the
realm of Pluto) can be restored. Barker suggests that romantic
love is dead in the age of scientific positivism. "Love" is the
word by which lust tries to hide its nature. The sweet singer has
lost his purity. He is betrayed and destroyed by passion.

In contrasting Orpheus to the Angels, Barker is no doubt allud-
ing to Rilke's distinction between the poet and the awe-inspiring,
self-sufficient "supreme creative power," the "divine antithesis to
natural man." [7] According to E. M. Butler, whose critical biography of Rilke Barker reviewed shortly before he wrote the elegies,[8]
the *Duino Elegies* are largely concerned with the crisis brought on
by the artist's striving to attain the supreme eternity of the "dai-
mon of poetical inspiration," who made human love seem inconsequential and ephemeral.[9] Barker had read Rilke earlier; a 1939
poem about him[10] and, of course, his assertion that all poems are
elegies attest to his interest. In Rilke's poems and in Butler's explanation, Barker must have found an analogue of his own poetic
problem of yearning for transcendence. Like Rilke, Barker finally

identified himself with the natural world where Orpheus was the god of poetry.

In "Satan is on your tongue" Barker associates the poet with Orpheus, high priest of Dionysus. He is not forgetting that Orpheus was killed by women—hence his justification for insisting that love is destructive. Although Barker's Orpheus is Dionysian (not the gentle, withdrawn Rilkean Orpheus), the frame of reference for Elegy III is surely Rilke's poetry.

The last two stanzas broaden the indictment of Orpheus and the lovers to all who hide their grief in the "five senses" to escape the horrors of a wrong-headed, rootless society:

> Marooned on the islands of pride, lonely
> And mad on the pyramids of achievement,
> Disillusioned in the cathedrals of doxology,
> The sad man senses his continual bereavement:
> God has just died, and now there is only
> Us. The gold bull with its horns of finances
> Over the sensual mountains goes gallivanting
> In Glory: all night and all day it dances,
> Absurd and happy because nothing is wanting.
> The sad man hides his grief in his five senses.

Nietzsche's parable of the death of God, with Pascal's vision of the greatness and misery of mankind, forms the background for the elegies. Within their framework, Nietzsche's pronouncement is the catastrophe of history. Man's isolation, alienation, and disillusionment reflect a crumbling culture. Deprived of a universe for which God provides the moral order, the individual is left with the terrible burden of responsibility. Modern man in an atheistic, materialistic age, like the people of Moses, worships an idol—the gold bull which appropriately suggests the false gods Barker denounces—materialism and sensuality.

Although Elegy III implies an existentialist attitude, it conveys only the horror of a despairing escapism. The poet accepts total freedom, confronts *angst,* despair, and crisis; but he is unable to wring from the absurd any promise of dignity. The suggestion that the failure of love is at the heart of the matter parallels, of course, a major theme of *The Waste Land.* But Barker's despair, like Rilke's, is first personal, then cosmic. The symbol of the poet merges with that of people in love, and both are absorbed in the powerful criticism of secular culture. Each part of the telescoping indictment contains its opposite and hence the sense of tension: Orpheus is contrasted to the Angels; love, to the necessary sexual satisfaction; and a world with God, to a Goddess society.

The mood of disillusionment carries over to "Secular Elegy IV" where neither science nor sensation discloses "the heart of the matter" or "truth." Man's direction is wrong: "we dissect for data" or lose ourselves "Under the frenzies of all sensual wonders." Thus

> in circles over existential deserts
> I and you wander, lost, and arm in arm;
> Lost, lost. And the visions paying us visits
> Lead us to mirages where, in a morning dream,
> We forget the headaches and lost Edens.

The "existential deserts" seem only to indicate the sterility and misdirection of modern thought; once more Barker cannot recognize the possibility of integrity in an atheistic society.

But the modern Romantic must devise a world outlook which can reconcile his feeling for the spiritual with the facts of the material world. The last two elegies climax the bitterly secular attitude which dominates the series and are clues to the meaning of the title of the volume. In defining dual aspects of the eternal female, a divinity like the spouse-mother Jung speaks of, they represent the dogma of Eros. In the somewhat ironic title *Eros in Dogma,* the juxtaposition of the pagan Eros to a word which usually refers to the doctrines of the church implies the poet's need for a system of belief. Eros refers at the same time to the Greek god of love and to the essentially selfish Freudian Eros which emerges in myth and ritual illustrating its ambivalent nature. Barker creates goddesses in sexual and familial terms: he personifies the erotic principle as a "nine-tiered tigress" (Elegy V) and the maternal principle as "mother of us all" (Elergy VI). Eros is the religion of the modern man who has dissected his soul and subjected it to the laws of biology and psychology. Although the Romantic sensibility is at war with the terrors of modern beliefs, at the same time it searches for sustenance in them.

The tigress of "O Golden Fleece" (V) is the archetypal fatal woman. Renderer of both pleasure and pain, she represents the

golden prize, the rich spoils which challenged Jason and Hercules
to bold and glorious deeds. Not simply a beautiful blonde woman,
she is nature herself. The opening apostrophe to her hair is, however, more than a symbol of beauty and fulfillment: the winning
of the fleece involved Medea's sorcery as well as Jason's heroism.
But the implications of sorcery are not immediately apparent in
the lovely first stanza:

> O Golden Fleece she is where she lies tonight
> Trammelled in her sheets like midsummer on a bed
> Kisses like moths flitter over her bright
> Mouth, and as she turns her head,
> All space moves over to give her beauty room.
> Where her hand, like a bird on the branch of her arm,
> Droops its wings over the bedside as she sleeps,
> There the air perpetually stays warm
> Since, nested, her hand rested there. And she keeps
> Under her green thumb life like a growing poem.

The similes surrounding this sleeping woman suggest her relationship to nature. The poem literally flowers in its implications; nature's life-giving, protective maternity is revealed as we view her
in repose.

But suddenly the poet contrasts to his word painting the violent
animal imagery of Stanza 3:

> My nine-tiered tigress in the cage of sex
> I feed with meat that you tear from my side
> Crowning your nine months with the paradox:
> The love that kisses with a homicide
> In robes of red generation resurrects.

The striking first image is in part explained by Barker himself in
his novel *The Dead Seagull:* "How much of our sudden aversion
for each other and as sudden love, comes from our having caged
ourselves together? And what we are caged in is, in the end, the
locked and barred box of zoological sex. . . . It is love that kills
us with the killer of sex" (80). Man is sustained by the sexual activity in which his pregnant, long-lived tigress, "mother Nature,"
forces him to indulge, thus engaging him in the cycles of genera-

tion that keep her "nine-tiered," perpetually ready to produce off-spring. Nature is "The imperial multiplicator nothing can nonplus"; destiny never worries her. Like Baudelaire's *Hymne a la Beauté*, Barker's poem asks which part of the dichotomy is real and essential: is nature (and female nature) "Ange ou Sirene?" According to Jung, the "mythological Great mothers" were voluptuous, devouring creatures who were usually "a danger to their sons." [11] Marsden, one of the three principal characters in *The Dead Seagull*, is the counterpart of the *femme fatale* in "O Golden Fleece," an amoral tigress.[12]

If Marsden is comparable to the female principle in Elegy V, Theresa (in the same novel) is comparable to the maternal saint in Elegy VI. Like Saint Theresa, she is a martyr of spiritual love. If Marsden is the body, Theresa is the soul of love.[13] If it were not a "secular" elegy, one might be tempted to interpret "Temper the Whirlwind" (Elegy VI) as a poem of Mariolatry, especially considering that it was written by a quondam Catholic interested in medieval literature. The Gnostics had set Mary up as the third part of the trinity. Barker's poem, like the Catholic "Hail, holy Queen," asks for mercy and pity for man in his unhappy state. The prayer says "To Thee do we cry, poor banished children of Eve; to Thee do we send up our sighs, mourning and weeping in this valley of tears." Barker writes "Large in your arms wrap our sad amalgam/That . . . /Mopes, lost and weeping, far far from its home."

In "Temper the Whirlwind" motherhood is exalted as a secular deity. Barker supplicates the "Mother of us all," Eve, to make things easier for the unborn child, the innocent "lamb." Maternal pity can "cover . . . the broken Pole" of the earth off its axis. The comparison to dirty "dishcloths" is perhaps justifiable in addressing so domestic a deity as a pregnant woman; man's pride is dirty as dishcloths. The archetypal mother is asked to keep man from understanding the ultimate mysteries of "Death and Truth," to take the lovers, her devotees, "to their last bed" when the due season arrives, and to help man bear up under the weight of the world:

> Let the mannikin Adam successfully undertake
> What Atlas only, bending an apish double.
> Hitherto managed with the world on his back.

References to the "shawls of cause" and to "The lovers who are the cause of all the trouble" suggest the paradox of foreordination and free will associated with original sin. The contradictions can be justified by Barker's insistence (Stanza 3) that human reason should not discover ultimate truth. Thus the speaker can finally supplicate the original mother once again to make things easier for the lamb—to give the young special advantages and luck (silver spoons) and to extend Love "to those who groom your bridal/ That they, mother of us all, suffer in your name." There is no resentment against the first mortal mother, although man suffers for her sin and at the same time has his moral nature because of her.

Unlike "O Golden Fleece," which is organized in terms of sharp contrast and reconciliation of opposites, "Temper the Whirlwind" might be said to have a circular structure and unity of tone. The archetypal mother, really agape personified in the female, dominates the poem which is permeated with the supplicant's sadness. The use of the vocative and the refrainlike repetitions in the first and last stanzas unify the poem. The form and devices are typical: Barker devised a quintaine written roughly in iambic pentameter or, perhaps more accurately, in sprung rhythm with five beats to a line. The rhyme scheme is *ababa* or a variation; the poet relies also on half rhyme, internal rhyme, and internal half rhyme. In the elegies Barker achieves the remarkable musical effects appropriate for their sad secularism.

III   *Elegies of Estrangement*

In 1941, when Denis de Rougemont's *Love in the Western World* was translated into English, W. H. Auden reviewed it in *Nation* in an essay entitled "Eros and Agape." [14] A few months later Barker began a series of reviews for *Nation,* and probably he had read Auden's review; if he had not already read de Rougemont's book, he no doubt read with interest this treatise on the difference between Romantic and Christian love. For Barker—who already suspected that love and carnality were closely allied, who saw the world in dualistic terms, and who longed for the infinite—de Rougemont's explanation of the Manicheanism at the heart of Western love would have given an ideological framework to what he had suspected all along. Barker's secular elegies V and VI reveal the influence. De Rougemont ends his book stressing that the failure to distinguish between Eros and Agape "causes the general breakdown of our European civilization. . . ." [15] The disaster is the victory of paganism, not the fault of Christianity.

That passion isolates and destroys is the first premise of the "Sacred Elegies." The titles suggest man's essential loneliness, and the primary theme of estrangement expands outward from the private world of lovers to society and finally to the metaphysical implications of private and public separation of man from God. The elegies are arranged in order of climax: "I. The Separation of Lovers"; "II. The Exile of the Traveller, the Poor and the Invalids"; "III. The Isolation of the Great and all Historical Isolation"; "IV. The Actual but Imperfect Union of the Lover, the Labourer and the Poet with the Object of their Love"; "V. The Separation of Man from God."

The melancholy, nostalgic "Sacred Elegy I" treats the clearly Romantic subject of separated lovers. "Sacred Elegy II," which develops out of the experience of the first poem, associates the imaginative fulfillment of dreaming of home with the only real peace that can be achieved—annihilation, or union with the Magna Mater, "The maternal/Mirage." The second deals, then, with the death wish, the wish for "the palatial womb"; it concludes with the invitation: "'Come to the womb, come, for it is home,'/O invalids in love and indigence, return/To the hands of stars and the universal bosom." Barker's desire springs less from longing for immortality than from disillusionment, for the explorer, the poor, and the invalid are all cut off from any hope of solace in life.

"The Isolation of the Great and all Historical Isolation" (Elegy III) develops even further the theme of isolation. It focuses on the alienating effects of ego on conscious supermen and, in effect, on contemporary society which has liberated itself from the past and hence achieved an estrangement more terrible than any of historical precedent. Napoleon, the prototype of the "giant egoists" of the past, exiled on St. Helena, gives an informed opinion of the dangers of rampant egoism. Barker's response to Napoleon, like that of former Romantics, moves from admiration to distrust. He chooses this empire builder as the voice of experience. Like Byron, he analyzes Napoleon as lacking any community of feeling with mankind.[16] Self-love is the denial of feeling for humanity.

From the perspective of history Napoleon can see the terrible situation in which "Caesar has been/Set snarling at large in the ethical arena./All law is down." The Caesar who creates moral anarchy is the modern demagogue:

> The conscious supermen, grinning in style,
> Wearing elected parliaments in their lapels,
> Gaze out of newspapers at all those peoples
> Who fight and believe and die under their smile.
> Sacred in crystal Stalin shall sleep and
> Be illegally illustrious. But at his foot
> The dachshund and the private diamond lie.
> Somewhere an Austrian corporal shall be mute
> At whose word once, from Europe to the sky,
> Suddenly everyone everywhere began to die.

Barker prophesies that Stalin will die and become "illegally illustrious. . . ." The poet suggests, moreover, the hypocrisy of the Marxist leader: Stalin has useless pets and private wealth, "The dachshund and the private diamond." He predicts, too, that Hitler will be silenced. These titans, "conscious" because at least Hitler justified himself as a Nietzschean superman, will be isolated if only by death.

A third kind of superman, the archetypal poet (Stanza III), is the lonely Byronic hero:

> The colossal Apollo. The sky-writer with
> Guilt in his thumbmark, the poet with the human
> Hanging at hand, cut with a verb to the nerve,
> Rabbits at butchers. The arrogant wreath
> Bright at his face, the Mephisthelean omen,
> Both wards away and draws a man and woman.

The impressionistic imagery suggests that the Romantic poet (Manfred-Faust-and the persona merged into one), wearing his laurels, destroys other people; but he is afraid to face wholesale slaughter. He "rabbits at butchers" such as the conscious supermen of Stanza II. Thinking no doubt of Byron (and perhaps of himself), the poet writes:

> O seeking at all altars a Sybilline to serve
> Either in beds or wars, he finds only

> The anthropoid I gibbering from mirrors. Lonely
> The poet walks among a score of selves.

Looking for oracular utterances on behavior in love or war, the
poet finds only himself. "Beds or wars" suggests the two central
experiences of Byron's life (and perhaps of Barker's)—a long record of amours and a fight against tyranny. Byron, like Barker,
created poems in which the central character or persona was almost invariably an aspect of himself.

The beginning of Stanza IV follows from the reference to
Byron; his heroes are aptly described in the first line: "Akimbo on
mountains the heroic egoist/With poems or murders or empires
in his pocket/May also remember Love." Typically, the lines
merge former references: they remind us of all the supermen—the
poems of "The colossal Apollo," the murders of Stalin and Hitler,
the empires of Caesar. But, like the Byronic hero, supermen are
lonely. Egoism isolates; their strength shuts them off from the only
real values, Love and human sympathy.

In the conclusion of the five-stanza elegy, Barker turns from the
"solitary heroes" to modern man who lacks the historical sense
(and has not learned, therefore, the dangers of pride). Barker
does not attempt to analyze the cause of our ironic freedom; the
words of the paradox, "Liberated independent we are lost," reveal, however, the central problem of a scientific age which has
cut man off from traditional certainties. Modern men are "The
scapegoat generation," for they take upon themselves the blame
that belongs to the past; yet they proudly refuse its lessons. Modern man is cut off in what Barker calls "historical isolation." Now
responsible for himself, he can only hope for a miracle—"But on
our own,/Clasping a spirit we walk water home." The last line
might seem a sudden departure were it not for the fact that separation by water forms a persistent theme in the "Sacred Elegies."
In the first two elegies isolation can be ended only by contact with
water. In Elegy III the connotation, reminding us of Christ walking on the water, is genuinely sacred; but "spirit" is not capitalized. The miracle is still a secular one which refers ambiguously to
the hope for some extraordinary event that would confute the
laws of nature, as well as to the doubt that it could happen. If
man walks water home in a world where water does not regener-
ate, he drowns. In the canon of the poems we recall that "home" is

the return to the womb water of the Magna Mater—that death is
the only end of alienation.

The love that the isolated egoists overlooked is explored further
in Elegy IV. Concerned with the union of opposites, it probes the
enigma of the presence of opposites in one another. Lovers are
joined in marriage or the kiss. "From an ark of isolation/The
beasts of love emerge in pairs and bring Hymenaeals here." But
this union reveals another, that of Eros and the death wish (II).
Death is present in life, especially in those whom self-love impris-
ons, in those never capable of giving themselves wholly: "Some
shall be most alone with a lover, never/Letting the sweating
hand unlock the closet of/The coffined I." Though the union is
actual, it is not real and satisfying. The spiritual union of lovers, of
the worker and his tools, or of the poet and the object is not
achieved. Death is the only release from unnatural unions and the
dialectic of union and divorce. The speaker invokes "Thanatos" as
the eternal home, the Being toward which he directs his true alle-
giance. The emergent Eros, apparently the soul of the lover,

> at last liberated from the individual,
> The solitary confinement of an evil lease,
> Returns to the perfect. Azrael, Azrael,
> Azrael enters with papers of pardon releasing
> The idiot poets from biological cells.

Azrael, the angel who separates the soul from the body at the
moment of death, releases the idealist from the prison of Becoming.

Eros' return to the perfect is the pagan equivalent of the "return
to God" in the powerful concluding elegy (V), "The Separation of
Man from God." This poem reiterates the motifs of the others.
The separation of lovers (Elegy I) is drawn in when God, "like
Love," reveals Himself "in absence"; the desire of the explorer, the
poor, and the invalid to go home to the universal bosom (II) is
suggested by "the desire in the heart of hearts/To come home to
you makes you most manifest"; the flaw of ego (III) is "ashes of
pride"; the imperfect unions in life (IV) are related to the paradox of Becoming "where/Ashes of pride on all the tongues of
sense/Crown us with negatives." This last refers obliquely to the
Ash Wednesday service where the Catholic's forehead is

"crowned" with ashes which remind him of his mortality and thus instill in him humility.

Man must, in fact, lose pride to have communion with God. Barker pleads for this self-effacement: "O deal us in our deserts/ The crumb of falling vanity. It is eucharist." The renunciation of pride is the means to making a new covenant with Christ; humility is essential to the sacrament. Barker asks, however, that humility be given like grace, without any real effort on the part of the supplicant. He does not proceed to it through the defeat of self so that he can say with Eliot in "Ash Wednesday," "Lord I am not worthy." It is the desire in the Romantic's own "heart of hearts" that most convinces him of God's existence.

Although God is separated from man, mankind moves toward Him (Stanza II). Accepting the age of scientific progress, men go toward Him in "geometrical progession," praising though they are dumb members of the chain gangs of life, accepting, even "hugging, the traumas" that modern psychology provides them as if they were "halleluias." All things (Stanza III) "moving in obedient machinery" seem to admit that God is the Creator:

> The great man dreaming on the stones of circumstances,
> The small wringing hands because rocks will not move:
> The beast in its red kingdom, the star in its arc:
> O all things, therefore, in shapes or in senses,
> Know that they exist in the kiss of his Love.

The kiss of Love is ironic in juxtaposition to the fact that the great and the small are alike tormented by hard circumstance.

Accepting the misery and contradictions of existence only hints at the bitterness of modern belief. Suddenly to the calm and detached irony of Stanza III is contrasted the fury of the final stanza:

> Incubus. Anaesthetist with glory in a bag,
> Foreman with a sweatbox and a whip. Asphyxiator
> Of the ecstatic. Sergeant with a grudge
> Against the lost lovers in the park of creation,
> Fiend behind the fiend behind the fiend behind the
> Friend. Mastodon with mastery, monster with an ache
> At the tooth of the ego, the dead drunk judge:
> Wheresoever Thou art our agony will find Thee

> Enthroned on the darkest altar of our heartbreak
> Perfect. Beast, brute, bastard. O dog, my God.

This stanza is not just magnificent blasphemy; it lays bare a terrifying moment of agonized and inverse acceptance. It cracks like a whip at the end of the poem and of the sequence. It reveals the enigmatic nature of a cruel, wrathful, irrational creature, a nightmare demon of the imagination, the evil spirit descending upon our sleep. God is horrifyingly real and so is the flagellant emotional response. Every inverted image concretizes Him. The poem speaks for the desperate acceptance of God's apparent evil and real perfection. In some ways, the poem is tantamount to religious conversion, although it is the violent epiphany of the self-sufficient Romantic who takes it upon himself to judge God or to recreate him in his own image. The new religion is Nietzsche philosophizing with a hammer, the Antichrist declaring war on the God he hates and envies, Baudelaire writing litanies to Satan, Shelley admitting God's existence but denying His benificence, or Blake condemning Him as cruel Nobodaddy.

Nonetheless, Barker might have written, like Pascal, "Je m'en suis séparé; je l'ai fui, renoncé, crucifié," before he experienced his moment of clarification. Barker has moved from the position of the "Secular Elegies" in which God was dead to the admission that He exists. In confronting the nothingness of secular existentialism, he finds God. The fragmented language and the short stabbing alliterative epithets of the last line underscore the anguish, almost the equivalent of the heartbreaking sobs of a metaphysical despair. Like Rilke, Barker blasphemes what he praises, marvels at what he believes essentially unlovable, and finally praises in spite of himself.

Like other tragic yea-sayers, Barker tries seriously to create a myth that will sustain his view of the world. The religion of Eros, however, proves an inadequate substitute for traditional Christianity. Eros herself is gradually subsumed into the framework of Neo-Platonism which in turn is easily subsumed into a somewhat heretical Christianity. In the canon of the poetry, it is clear that the catastrophe at which the elegies arrive in the savagely tormented final stanza of "the Separation of Man from God" is not so much a denial as an admission of God, though He may be the God of Gnosticism.

In a very real sense, then, the elegies arrive at a tragic affirmation. Like all tragedy, they concern the problems of evil and of man's destiny. Like Oedipus, the persona is a protagonist in conflict with circumstance; and his search for clarification leads to a dilemma and finally to catastrophe. The dramatic structure develops to a climax in the final secular elegies where the persona makes a choice between two evils—a godless amoral universe or a moral order activated by a cruel divinity. From the point when he supplicates the Magna Mater, the untying of the knot and final cracking of the whip are only matters of time. The disaster—man's estrangement from God—paradoxically reasserts the dignity of man.

Forced to recognize the supreme authority, at the moment of recognition, the protagonist declares his freedom by the very act of defiance. He could, like Oedipus, say that the hand that struck him was his own. He achieves tragic dignity and the tragic realization which prefaces it. What Barker finally says is no less agonized than Gloucester's statement in *King Lear:* "As flies to wanton boys are we to the gods; they kill us for their sport." The sense of God's remoteness and indifference, of the world's rank evil, and yet of faith in man, who despite his inability to control the "stones of circumstance," can understand his fate and, understanding it, can accept it by defying it—these are the elements of tragedy that Aristotle says purge us through pity and fear; and these are also the elements of Barker's powerful poems which, read as a sequence, indeed call for tragic catharsis.

Closely related to the final Sacred Elegy is "Dog, Dog in my Manger," published in Oscar Williams' *A Little Treasury of Modern Poetry* in 1946, but not printed in either *Eros in Dogma* or in *The Collected Poems.*[17] The title suggests the commonplace meaning of the term "Dog in the Manger"—one who is discontented and the cause of discontentment in others. The dog in the speaker's manger is, as Oscar Williams' section heading suggests, a shape of conscience. The controlling symbol is equivalent to the inverted God image of the final line of Elegy V. In Freudian terms, the later poem might be said to work out the relationship of the Superego and the Id; in Christian terms, the relationship of the angel and beast in man. The persona urges the dog to "drag at my heathen heart" to keep him from too much passion or from masochism. He asks the dog to help him to moderate his vices, to "guide my stray [because I am a stray canine, made in the Dog image] down quiet roads/Where peace is—be my engine of myth," to help him to understand the paradox of pleasure and pain and of good and evil.

Despite a narrower frame of reference, the seemingly contradictory conclusion is something like the end of the final elegy:

> Dog, dog, your bone I am, who tear my life
> To tatterdemalion from me. From you I have no peace,
> No life at all unless you break my bone,
> No bed unless I sleep upon my grief
> That without you we are too much alone,
> No peace until no peace is a happy home:
> O dog, my god, how can I cease to praise!

The ambiguity of "Dog, dog" lies in the lower-case god, presumably because God may be discovered in the depths of man's being. Charged with the emotional dynamic of spiritual struggle, the poem suggests both John Donne's "Batter My Heart Three Personed God" and Francis Thompson's "Hound of Heaven," which the modern poet openly admires and which might have provided him with his dog symbol.

IV   *The Antinomies of Love*

The emphasis on passion in "Dog, Dog, in my Manger" and the stress on Eros in the elegies foreshadow the subject matter of the "Love Poems"—the poet's ambivalent attitude toward love. In terms of the theme of *Eros in Dogma,* we move from the general to the particular scene. The love poetry suggests the individual fate as the manifestation of something larger. Although they celebrate childbirth, fulfilled sexual love, and domestic relations, they deal largely with guilty love. Like Byron, Barker might write, "My injuries came down on those who loved me." Significantly in terms of the somewhat Gnostic tone of *Eros in Dogma,* the series included in *Love Poems* (1947) and in *Collected Poems* as the third cycle is omitted from the 1944 volume: the group contains some of Barker's most positive statements about love.

In the first poem of this group, April, instead of being the cruel-
lest month, is the time of birth and fecundity when, "The dead
gods get up and rejoice/At circumventing death:/And to all these
I join my voice/In Love, Elizabeth." Despite the troubles of the
heart, the "antinomies,/The angel and the anthropoid," make love
across a void and "Kiss in a shower of pities" (II). "Nature, cradling kind in her arm,/Extends" love to all things in her care
(IV). Clearly these are chastened expressions of attitudes in the
elegies. "Shut the Seven Seas against Us" (III) could, however,
almost be mistaken for a nineteenth-century lyric; directly and
economically, it treats man's transciency and the consolations of
nature and love.

The "First Cycle of Love Poems" contains the most affirmative
poetry in *Eros in Dogma*. The first poem, "This morning take a
holiday from unhappiness," celebrates the birth of a son and
achieves unity and focus from a comparison to Christ's nativity.
But the four poems which follow are written from a passive, feminine point of view which stresses the pleasure-pain paradox of
passion. In Poem II the speaker wishes the lover to "Be over me
dominant" and associates pleasure with pain: "Sesame is on his
tongue and the unicorn rages/Round the abdominal amphithea-
tre." Without remorse, the persona relates sex to violation:

> Then here in my heart he lies as dark as pillage
> Where in my arms I hold
> The murderer who, Samsoning up my five pillars,
> Lies quiet now, for here at my heart I fold him.

The murderer of Poem II is also a creator. Poem III is a tribute
to the lover as creator, a god in the universe of the feminine
speaker. The electrifying sexual experience contains the elements
of the pleasure-pain motif: "Lightning cracks my face of heaven."
Masculine passion is a "flammenwerfer" which connotes the intensity of the emotion, as well as the phallus and the power to devas-
tate. The sinful nature of sex is suggested with "The kiss is maypole where my seven/Happiest sins truss me to the rod." The kiss
celebrates May Day rites of spring and fertility; the rod or maypole is, of course, phallic. The speaker is fastened closely, the passive victim of happy and painful passion. Poem IV continues to
expound on the antimony of love:

> So he looks out over my subjugation
>   Where the combers coil at his feet,
> And sees, the far side of adulation,
> My hesperides rise singing, one moment, from the ocean
>   And the next, sinking, weep.

On the far side of the sexual paradise one weeps. The aquatic imagery points to the violence of the sexual act: "The narwhal with a spike on its brow/Spins thrashing through the wave:/His love is mine, who lashes now/In the sweat of seas I gave."

"My joy, my jockey, my Gabriel" (V), a love poem whose very movement from excitement to calm is a correlative for the sexual act, chooses as a phallic symbol the serpent which connotes also the evil of sex. Like other erotic poems, it is fraught with Freudian sex symbolism. "My dragonfly roaring your engines" (Cycle II: III) is clearly dominated by the phallic symbol. After glorifying coitus, it considers separation. Although Barker tries to unify the poem by considering that the insect going "up through the shower" can produce the rainbow which will sustain and unite the lovers, the metaphysical image disintegrates into "tang at your tongue my thousand-mile kiss,/And the babe at the breast." At his best, as in "My joy, my jockey, my Gabriel," Barker uses a sustaining central column of associations or a unifying symbol.

Nature informs several love poems. The Second Cycle, from a male point of view, looks to nature for a parallel to motherhood (I), then treats the family relationship of infant daughter, mother, and male (II). The second poem effectively uses the pathetic fallacy; nature will watch over her child sleeping at the mother's breast "at the waterfall." All nature becomes the child's family: "The pine like father," "the Rockies' bosom," "The Okanegan [*sic*] Valley shall grave/Canada round your cradle." Finally, in this atmosphere of pagan animism, the father wishes charms of good fortune on the natural child.

Some of the love poems are unified by the symbols of Christian martyrdom. "And in your hand, with tears for water" (Second Cycle: IV) treats love-pain, martyrdom-guilt antinomies in terms of three constituents—Greek myth, architecture, and martyrdom. "I nailed on wood by her eyes" (Third Cycle: V) begins with the martyrdom theme. But, although the guilty Byronic lover is often implicitly aware of the religious problem, profane love is the dominant subject. "By those shallows where once Sorrow was" (Second Cycle: V) presents in largely secular terms the lover haunted by lost love. He remembers "Squalid with loss" the sorrowful end of love and his late love's "eyes bitter with/Obituaries like blinds." The end of love is a disaster which leaves the speaker prepared for anything: "Whatever the disaster asks/I give it, heart and all. O happy suicidal!" The Promethean lover is tortured by memory: "The eagle kills me"; and, when love is wrong, "existence is wrong."

In "Leaning in the evenings, I live" (Second Cycle: VIII), the speaker is again tormented by memory: "The dogs of memory, howling, shall/Mourn on the steps of the heart." He is haunted by "The spectre in a glass sepulchre/With a child on its arm," probably a framed photograph of wife and child; but, of course, sepulchre suggests physical death and the entombment of love. The Byronic theme is even more obvious in "My tall dead wives with knives in their breasts" (Third Cycle: I). The speaker, persecuted by feelings of guilt, could, like Manfred, say, "my embrace was fatal." He wants to expiate his sin through suffering: "Then let me gather/Nothing but vipers to my satisfactions." Nonetheless, he doesn't expect to forego satisfactions or to express the change of heart necessary for repentance.

"Less the dog begged to die in the sky" (Third Cycle: IV) portrays the cruel lover who, with mingled pleasure and pain obvious in the choice of words, gave his "sweet stark one" the "knife in the breast," which seems to refer to his unfaithfulness: "The long lie, the lying worm in the bed,/The cheat I attest." The speaker assumes the burden of guilt by comparing her to natural phenomena victimized by the whims of the gods or of man:

> Less the dog begged to die in the sky
>   Immortal and transfixed,
> Or the tall tree to grow on ground
>   Later axed and annexed,
> Than my dark one, my sweet stark one,
>   Begged the knife in the breast,
> The long lie, the lying worm in the bed,
>   The cheat I attest.
> But bull without a bell I trod
>   Among her mysteries,

> Simpleton with a bomb I hid
>   Shivering in her caves;
> And her hand came down out of a cloud,
>   Her beauty from the shadows
> Emerged and suffered what I did
>   To mitigate my sorrows.

She was less responsible for his cruelty than was Sirius, who became the dog star when Diana lamented her fatal error in killing Orion by placing him and his innocent dog "in the sky/Immortal and transfixed"; the woman wanted to be destroyed by love even less than a tree wants to be axed. Like these objects representing the heavens and nature, she bore the victimization with passive acceptance, while the speaker, with no check for his actions, used her to escape his own problems. The comparisons reveal her innocence and his bestial, irrational behavior. The pleasure-pain motif is clear; the obvious erotic symbols—the knife, worm, bull, bomb, caves—help to unify the poem as do the contrasting comparisons, the two similes for the woman in the first quatrain and the two metaphors for the man in the third. This controlled lyric expresses with clarity, compression, and the musical effects that Barker had learned to create, the guilt feelings of the Byronic lover.

V   *The Matter and the Manner*

The love lyrics reflect the struggle between what is and what should be—between the poet's conviction of the baseness of sexual desire and its glory, of the basic feelings of attraction and repulsion in the male and female whose "opposites wed" (Third Cycle: VI), or of the tension of separation for those who dream "distance gone . . . no longer lonely we sleep as the wide seas divide." The poems move between antitheses or balance tensions. The language is often highly ambiguous and paradoxical, the symbols predominantly Freudian and sensual. Despite the violent wrenching of language which underscores "the expense of spirit in a waste of shame," the love poems reveal many refinements of style.

Although *Eros in Dogma* contains flamboyant language and rebellious passion, Barker succeeds in giving a shape to his wildness. Still willing to use latinate, abstract language, he finds ways

of effectively combining it with the concrete; he knows what he is
doing when he speaks of islands of pride and pyramids of
achievement. He shapes some of his finest poems with symbols
such as the dog, the *femme fatale*, the Magna Mater, or Eros.
Pagan mythology, Christianity, and history inform the poems just
as much as modern psychology does. Despite the inclusion of Orpheus, Dionysus, Apollo, Atlas, and Venus, biblical and historical
imagery is pervasive. Such allusions underscore the subject of the
middle poetry—man in a state of crisis, both political and spiritual, for which the poet seeks the cause and cure.

As he seeks a resolution for the dilemmas of modern man, he
resolves conflicts more and more within the discipline of conventional form. In the "Love Poems" the refining process is perhaps
most evident. The search for directness and for metrical and stanzaic form is clear in a domestic lyric such as "O tender under her
right breast," where Barker writes ballad stanzas:

> The silver spoon and the one-eyed man,
>   The rabbit's foot and the clover,
> Be at your bed, from morning till
>   As now, the day is over.

Even here the repeated symbols for good luck indicate that, although Barker is pruning his style, he still writes extensively as
well as intensively. In fact, a more typical example of the middle
poetry is the final driving stanza of "The Separation of Man from
God" in which Barker catalogues epithets. Everywhere the style is
rich and the subject matter is compelling commentary on the
times. He frequently juxtaposes antitheses and unifies poems
through associational patterns which reflect a dominantly emotional response to private and public events. He draws the whole
world into himself, creating a dramatic, empathetic poetry. He
transforms personal suffering and disillusionment into powerful
poems.

CHAPTER 6

The Fifties :
The Feral Man Contending With the Sun

NEWS of the World (1950) reveals little significant change in Barker's subject matter. He is still preoccupied with love, still moved by the sad state of the world; he is increasingly aware of the people who form his literary milieu. The mood of pessimism and estrangement dominates. When this mood is translated within the limits of personal experience, the poetic product is sometimes very fine indeed.

I News from a Nightmare World

The "Bridal Nightmare" poems are complicated, but successful because form reflects the hallucinatory internal experience which is their subject; and even the title reveals the contradictory nature of love. "The Bridal Nightmare I" centers in the consciousness of a bride and bridegroom whose mutual misery is revealed:

> Nightmare in whose arctic wings
>   Lifelong I unmoving lie
> Folded your cold heart I sleep
> And hear the wrong-faced children weep
>   Outside in uncharity.
> Bridal nightmare, sheeted, stained,
> Broken, now, is that vain idol
> Bespoken bridegroom I beside.
> That cracked cup, an empty heart
> Fell away and, from my hand,
> Slipped lie and poison on my pillow,
> Lie lifelong here at my left side,
> Unspeaking and unspoken bride
> For every side we lie beside
> Satisfies and is satisfied.
> Unbridled nightmare, day bedfellow,
> I am my nightmare, awake, asleep;

Creep out, creep out, cold man, and comfort
The wrongs where they weep!

Inverted sytnax and ellipsis help to convey the fragmented experience of a bad dream and of the double awareness Barker tries to
capture. The nightmare is shared by the "Bespoken bridegroom"
and the "unspoken bride," whose bridal has been solemnized
in the eyes of God alone. The bride's nightmare results from the
loss of her virginity and of her illusions about her lover. "Sheeted,
stained/Broken" reveal the loss of maidenhead; "stained" suggests, moreover, that she has been corrupted or stigmatized with
guilt by the act. The "vain idol" may be her virginity; it may also
be her lover. Sexual experience brings disillusionment.

The man's nightmare overlaps the woman's. He thinks of her as
a cracked cup, easily defined as the violated womb. When he releases her, the emptiness and falsity of the relationship are plain;
he assumes guilt is recognizing the "lie and poison" of the act. Because she has been despoiled, "fell away" is appropriate; at the
same time, the sin itself is released and recognizable. He acknowledges the failure of love: "every side we lie beside/Satisfies and
is satisfied," for the sexual act is simply a necessary satisfaction.
The experience that promised ecstatic fulfillment provides only
duplicity and injury. The sense of disenchantment and wrong is
fused in the packed form, which approximates the interlocking of
internal monologues.

Guilt is the theme of the haunting lyric "The Bridal Nightmare
II" which might aptly be called "Turn, turn away your face." At
first, this complex poem seems to treat the martyrdom of love, a
major concern in the "Love Poems." Superficially, it seems to compare the crucifixion to the ennoblement of the suffering partner in
love:

The kiss is diagonals on which you die
Smiling in sweat because
The turn of your face away would undo
The cross of a kiss.

The kiss that crucifies seems to indicate that "you" is the partner
in love for whom the sexual act is pleasure and pain. This interpretation is not, however, so convincing when we look at stanza
three which says "it is *you* who are glittering like a star and/*We*

who are dead" (italics mine). There is a third person in the poem, one removed from the actual lovemaking. The possibility of three or more members of the dramatis personae is increased with "Who rubs our double death together . . . /So that we shed the fire, the child, and each other?" Had the poet capitalized "you," the interpretation would clearly concern Christ and His perpetual suffering over man's continued sinfulness; but, in doing so, Barker would have sacrificed the ambiguity which purposefully plays on the likeness of Christ to a forsaken loved one, present in spirit or in the conscience of the speaker as he sins with another lover. Finally, the poem concerns the Byronic conflict of remorse without repentance and the paradox of belief in both Christ and "procreative fate."

The poem is, then, addressed to Christ who suffers for us each time we reenact the sexual sin—and Christ is momentarily identified with the female victim "Smiling in sweat." Comments in *The Dead Seagull* and in *The True Confession of George Barker* fortify and amplify this interpretation. The material in the novel sounds like a commentary: "Physical love is a sin because there . . . god has been rendered unnecessary. . . . the blasphemy of two lovers, at that mutually sufficient moment of consummated love, when god, standing in the corner of the room, knows that, at the kiss, he is unnecessary, this is the blasphemy that drives him, no matter how briefly, out of our house" (101). One stanza of the confession refers to this poem:

> I confess, my God, that in
>   The hotbed of the monkey sin
> I saw you through a guilt of hair
>   Standing lonely as a mourner
> Silent in the bedroom corner
>   Knowing you need not be there:
> I saw the genetic man had torn
>   A face away from your despair. (35)

The kiss that is double death is torture to the One who assumed the burden of sin for man. Since He is all powerful, His turning away from man would undo the meaning of the original crucifixion, would invalidate it, and would leave man to the amoral state of the beasts or bring him to the Day of Judgment. When He no longer looks on man, hoping that His faith in him will be justified,

the notions of sin and expiation will no longer exist: "The turn of
your face away would undo/The cross of a kiss."

The fact that He witnesses the act, if only in the mind of the
sinner, makes it a perpetual martyrdom:

> Who locked you in the shuddering
> Rock that will rot and die
> The day that you turn your suffering
> Face away?
>
> Who fixed you in the form
> From which, ghost in a wall,
> You look out on the workings of a will that
> Forgives us all.
>
> Who pinned you on a crossroad where
> With bright limbs spread
> It is you who are glittering like a star and
> We who are dead?

The final stanzas reiterate the guilt feelings inspired by illicit sex
and imply that it is Christ who is shamed as He witnesses what we
blame on procreative fate:

> Who rubs our double destruction together
> Save procreative fate
> So that we shed the fire, the child, each other?
> Turn, turn away your face!

The "shade," really akin to Hopkins' "immortal diamond" although
modern man has hidden Him, matters; but He does so negatively
through man's guilt. The state of the criminal lover is almost as
discouraging as that of the martyr. Man is the tool of his sexual
nature, the flint which produces the fire of passion which we
throw off, along with the child, who is product of the act. After
momentary physical union, the lovers shed each other like gar-
ments or water. The speaker utters his desire to escape his lament-
able state or to counteract his conscience with the ironic. "Turn,
turn away your face." The persona has free will and moral responsibility ("I with a hand of guilt laid stone"), and yet he is bound
by the dictates of the Freudian Eros.

The ambivalent controlling image and paradoxical content of
"The Bridal Nightmare II" contribute to the organic unity. The

tension in the modern mind that is unable to disentangle the emotional claims of body and spirit remains unresolved. The form is dialectical. Even the quatrains with their long third lines and three, four, or five syllabled fourth lines which rein in the movement of the third, create the sense of urgency, emphasis, and finally of suspension which are important to the total effect. In resolving the conflict in the pattern of the poem, Barker uses the oxymoron and ambiguity because the experience itself is contradictory and ambivalent. "The Bridal Nightmare II" discloses the poet on a religious tether; he is affirming, while he tries desperately to deny Christ.

"The Bridal Nightmare III" treats the pain of love once more in a religious context. The imagery refers to the fall of man and to the Abraham and Isaac story in order to suggest the destructiveness of love, which produces "the purgatory Babe in the pride of the abandoned bride." The speaker would sacrifice his child on the altar of his ego. He is persecuted by memory of the original sin which Barker almost invariably associates with sex: "Bright snakes in the shadows/Hiss the wicked story/And the apple is struck and resounds like a gong/In the cuts of the misery." Eve's contemporary counterpart has undergone the temptation and fall and also the curse of pain in childbirth. Her babe, illegitimately conceived or deserted, a soul bound for purgatory, must through suffering pay his parents' debt with temporal punishment; he must enter the purgatory of life.

The poem, developing through the free associations of a hallucinatory dream, moves from the temptation to the speaker's apparent desertion of the bride because her injured ego "cried out/ Out:" The modern Eve doesn't use her charms to get her Adam to share her sin, and he doesn't stand by her, probably because he identifies himself simultaneously with the snake tempter and with her lover. His jealousy, like a snake coiled around a stone, "Cuddling the cold stone of a green-eyed ego" (faintly suggesting both Othello and Milton's Satan), would like to sacrifice the bride and the innocent lamb to the sense of wounded ego. The speaker's sense of guilt and of impending doom ("Judgments build up in the west") grows as "I . . . Die night by night." The erotic implications of die, borrowed from the seventeenth-century metaphysical poets, are especially appropriate; the word reflects the contradictory nature of the procreative act.

"Bridal Nightmare III" is not simply the hallucinatory dream of a Byronic lover. The speaker suffers because of an act of will. He feels the curse because he has reiterated the original sin (as Barker interprets it); he has premeditated the deed: "I was left alone . . . I watched you . . . I lifted the axe. . . ." He suffers the consequences. His suffering is the nightmare of remembering the deed and its archetype; his guilt is the poem, whose irrational imagery and organization reflect his torment.

The culpable Cain is a central figure in *News of the World*. In "Sestina at 34" the persona says life is a "journey of hazard and heroes, monster and blizzard." "Zennor Idyl I" asserts that "The monster in a storm/Is always I." "Zennor Idyl II" laments,

> And in the wild
> Winds of memory, then, great thistles toss
> Their hair and lash the recollection
> Till the granite that groans inside us weeps.

Barker's persona rages against "the pricks that drive/Me and my guardian out of house./I hear the worm and ghost connive/Coldly against me. I survive/By fathering monsters I abuse." Later he says, "Shame is my mark."

The Byronic hero wills his misdeeds, but sometimes Barker is not so convinced of our freedom. In "On the Approaching Birth of a Child to Friends," the poet cries, "We are automata." In "To My Son" he advises his own child that

> She and I
> Shall always meet when all wishes
> Under the dazzle of unpropitious
> But irresistible ascendencies.
> Clasp each other because they freeze.

The sexual pull is magnetic. The female

> Saw fate had taught her
> That she was an elected daughter
> And in obedience to the pull
> Of that which knows it is beautiful
> I moved towards her in the cold
> And fell into a moon. The golden
> Undergrowth of her sex enmeshed

> The dying fugitive it refreshed
> For henceforward daily dying.
> Sucking blood a Venus, sighing,
> Toys her prey back into life:
> He rules her with the sexual knife
> That kills him.

We are once more in the context of pleasure and pain which informs the Golden Fleece elegy. The female is an irresistible *femme fatale*, especially to the male who allows ego to stultify his will:

> Know nothing, sweet son and green lamb,
> Of the satanic 'I am'
> That opens up a rock of wrath
> And shows us the golden path
> To that glass palace where Love
> Keeps her prize pigs.

Sexual love is the Circean enchantress, the epitome of sin. Nonetheless, in "To My Son" Barker reaches out to define a paradoxical affirmation which underlies his most mature thought:

> Underneath
> The human heart, I believe,
> Lives a god who cannot grieve
> No matter how disastrous
> The crimes our passion brings on us
> Because this ungrieving god
> Knows that either bad or good
> Might look, from a better angle,
> Like a double-headed angel.

This god looks from the heights beyond good and evil to assert that they are really aspects of the same thing. The dialectic concerns good and evil, innocence and experience. An epistolary poem of advice from father to son, skillfully presented in conversational tetrameter couplets is a particularly appropriate vehicle for contrasting innocence and experience and for concluding that the real justice "Exacted on us" is in the acts to which passion drives us while we still "remember what innocence was." Nostalgia for the guilelessness of childhood marks Barker's Romanticism.

With the directness, the simplicity, and the music that typify Barker's later work, the lyric "Summer Song I" reiterates the theme of lost innocence. Borrowing from Sir Philip Sydney, the speaker looks into his "heart to write," but he finds a "desert there." Out of this contrast the conclusion develops:

> My one, my one, my only love,
>   Hide, hide your face in a leaf,
> And let the hot tear falling burn
> The stupid heart that will not learn
>   The everywhere of grief.
>
> Great summer sun, great summer sun,
>   Turn back to the never-never
> Cloud-cuckoo, happy, far-off land
> Where all the love is true love, and
>   True love goes on for ever.

The yearning for "cloud-cuckoo" joy and guiltlessness, before the lovers in the first garden hid their nakedness in leaves, is expressed in this song with clarity and with the metrical perfection which Barker commands in his mature work when he isn't more interested in expressing ideas than emotions.

"The Five Faces of Pity" is a poem intent on clarifying ideas. The serious religious theme is suggested even in the basic use of terza rima, probably borrowed from Dante. Each of the five sections dealing with the "five faces" contains sixteen lines. The speaker prays for faith to believe in things unseen and indicates that "Division exists only to prove who loves." Man, separated from the infinite so that he can prove his faith, has pushed the vision of pity out. The third section questions: "May it not, somehow, become fatal for all those/Who have solicited the various adverse powers/To advance them in an unforgivable purpose . . . ?"

After asking for pity for all the alienated people who were the subjects of the "Sacred Elegies," he sets up the dichotomy of love and pity. Love is equated with passion or Eros and pity with Agape. Love is masculine; Pity, "his sister." Love destroys; pity redresses. The preacher interferes with the poet, and the purposes of argument weaken the poem. The abstract, moral terminology, redundant supplication to the feminine divinity, and baldly stated paradoxes ("What love destroys, pity always restores") are ineffectual devices for communicating emotion. As prayer, the poem may succeed; as poetry, it fails. At best, it indicates without benefit of metaphor the direction of Barker's thought.

Although "The Weepers in the Sacred Tree" is a poem of interrogation rather than supplication, like "The Five Faces of Pity," it deals with the religious categories, with the abstractions "destiny . . . virtue . . . peace," and with the overwhelming question "Why do we live at all?" Although the poem treats ultimates, it achieves organic unity through the central symbol of the tree of life out of which speaks anguished humanity:

> 'O brute and hour, tooth and knife,
>   Condemned to live and suffer and never die
> Pronounce the unholy Why.
>   Root out the assent at the source of life!'

Despite everything, the universe cannot give "A stellar negative." And so the world goes on, embracing humanity in the sacred tree of life. The poet reveals himself as the tragic yea-sayer.

II   *The Literary Supplement*

Even in his personal poems Barker suffers the burden of the mystery of existence. In sonnets to Hopkins and Baudelaire, printed side by side almost as companion poems, he wishes to be converted by Hopkins' "incomprehensible message," but he recognizes his attraction to Baudelaire's "inverted golgotha." He asks Hopkins for what seems to be more than the usual stylistic influence. But for its weak conclusion the sonnet, "To Father Gerard Manley Hopkins, S.J.," would be a remarkable achievement:

> Overhead on a wing under heaven, treading
>   Bright verbs on silence, writing red on hereafter,
> He is for ever his feathers on sunset shedding,
>   Bedding all beautiful in the far harder and softer
> Breath of his word, bird in a thrash alighting
>   All claws for the world that its heart is after,
> The wide wonder that, into his talon of writing,
>   Rose up, eyes open, to meet her emasculate master.
>
> Father of further sons who wear your plumage
>   For the good glory of the word, I speak for

All of us who inherit any merit of your image:
O long-faced convert, look down and seek for
　　Worthiness in one of us, and let him speak
　　Evangelizing the incomprehensible message.

The octave, informed by Hopkins' "The Windhover," merges the
Jesuit poet and the bird. It contains the sprung rhythm, the alliteration, the internal and end rhyme, even the sweeping dynamic
of Hopkins' description of the falcon's flight. And Barker too is
referring to the "achieve of, the mastery of the thing"; but the
achievement he describes is Hopkins' ability to seize so vividly
upon the world as his subject. After the powerful octave, the
sestet, which has none of the individuation Hopkins admired,
suffers by comparison.

"To Charles Baudelaire," a better unified sonnet, reveals that,
although the message of Hopkins is "incomprehensible," Barker
understands Baudelaire's litanies of Satan. "Les Litanies de Satan"
in *Les Fleurs du Mal* suggests the god of Baudelaire, the "Prince
de l'exil" to whom he prays, the "Baton des exiles, lamp des inven-
teurs." Barker is thinking of this inverted religiosity which Eliot
claims is backdoor Christianity.[1] Recognition of the speaker's kinship comforts him when he feels most lost; he asks Baudelaire to
"Walk with me." Although Barker could never be accused of Dan-
dyism, he frequently accuses himself of Satanism and nowhere
more clearly than in the Baudelaire sonnet:

　　　　　　　　　　　　　　　　I serve
　　Much the same master. Was your good a god?
　　I hate my ruler because he will not break me
　　Under the overloving justice of his rod,
　　Thus for but love I hate him. Take me
　　To that inverted golgotha you trod
　　And, O Sir, show me the mirror that will break me!

Baudelaire wrote that "evil is capable—not indeed of uplifting
one—but perhaps of adding to one's stature." [2] The mirror is the
reflection of self that the artist plunges into, "the trumped up
altar" of self-worship and at the same time "the mirror of art." [3]
Baudelaire wrote that "true progress—that is to say, moral progress—can occur only within the individual, and by his own
effort";[4] "God is a scandal—a scandal that spreads";[5] "The main

thing is to be a 'great man' and a 'saint' to *oneself*;[6] and such a man "should live and sleep in front of a mirror." [7] Barker wants to eat of the fruit of the tree of knowledge from which Baudelaire's "serpent spirit" is "untwined." He wants to gain humility, even if by the upsidedown method of searching for the self in art. He needs to lose himself to find himself—to find "the mirror that will break me." Significantly, his line seems to refer to art and to the self rather than to God.

Although sometimes contradictory, Barker's course is always dynamic and masculine. He can respect but never fully sympathize with the way of T. S. Eliot. In his "Verses for the 60th Birthday of Thomas Stearns Eliot," Barker asserts the difference:

> I never know the juggernauts
> Go bulldozing through my thoughts
> So that everything I own
> Is trod down and overthrown
> Without remembering that worse
> Than thunder in the hearse
> Is the supernatural sigh
> Of illusions as they die—
> But in the room of Eliot
> The visions whistle as they rot.

And later, in lines somewhat suggestive of Auden:

> Outside the huge negations pass
> Like whirlwinds writing on the grass
> Inscriptions teaching us that all
> The lessons are ephemeral;
> But as the huge negations ride
> And deprecate all things outside
> His window, he puts out his hand
> And writes with whirlwinds on the ground
> Asseverations that tame
> The great negations with his name.

Barker is partly in awe of his mentor, but gently critical of what he considers an escape from the conflict of existence. Barker admires vitality.

He particularly admired Michael Roberts, editor of *New Signatures* and a noteworthy poet himself. When Roberts died in 1948,

Barker wrote his "Elegy on the Death of Michael Roberts." The indelible impression their first meeting left on the younger man informs the poem. In his essay "Coming to London" Barker vividly recalls "that glacial machine of transfiguration, the masculine intelligence, in its most brilliant operations." [8] In the light of this adulatory description, the bombast of Barker's opening rhetorical question is perhaps forgivable: "How dare the greatest die?" This interrogation beginning the first and last stanzas gives the impression, however, that Roberts died purposely to affront the world and his admirers. It is an unnecessary contradiction of what Barker later clarifies—that "So wasteful the world is with her few of best."

But, generally speaking, Barker succeeds in capturing Roberts' enthusiasms, his personality, his ideas, and even his physical appearance in this memorial poem. In the preface to Michael Roberts' *Collected Poems*, his wife Janet writes that "Michael's personality was as clearly outlined as his face—lean, hawk-nosed. . . ." [9] Barker too recalls "that eagled head" and his "aquiline skull." He exploits the close connection between Roberts' love of mountain climbing and his idealism (his poems often contain climbing images that stand for spiritual ascent):

> O pinnacles where the elected princes die
> With their dogstar boots on and a truth in hand,
> O tabernacles glittering to attest
> So few have ever ascended so far or so high,
> O Michael's bone enshrined in altitude,
> Truth is meridian to tempt kings to try.

Roberts' wife writes, "He cared passionately about truth." [10] Barker refers to "the principle of right," the "noumena," [11] and Roberts' ability to "Talk through the truth like a ship through the sea." Finally, in order to declare Roberts' immortality in typical elegiac tradition, Barker asserts that Roberts lives as the inspiration for poetry.

III   *The Range and Style*

The most significant news of *News of the World* is the recurrence of the struggle with belief, a struggle which the poet is increasingly able to control within conventional poetic form. The range of experimentation with traditional structure is notable; he writes a sestina, sonnets, variations on the quatrain and quintain, terza rima, and tetrameter couplets. The formal requirements of verse concern him far more than they did in the early and in the middle work. Although "Sestina at 34" uses the six-line stanza and the six unrhymed end words of the sestina, Barker varies the elaborate scheme of the traditional form by beginning each stanza with the end word of line two of the preceding stanza; the pattern he creates is less elaborate than that of the original sestina. In his sonnets, he almost invariably exchanges the traditional iambic pentameter for an approximation of sprung rhythm; and he uses the rhyme scheme that suits his purposes. A preference for the ballad measure characterizes the lyric poems. When he wishes, however, to create a vigorous line to contain his growing cynicism or his need for conversational directness or forceful masculine argument, he turns, like Auden, to the tetrameter couplet which he uses skillfully in "Verses for the 60th Birthday of Thomas Stearns Eliot" and in "To My Son."

The subject matter is often personal—about the single persona of the Romantic poet. Some of the love lyrics are less complex than the "Bridal Nightmares"; the lovely "Turn on your Side and Bear the Day to Me" celebrates the beauty and importance of the loved one. There are purely exploratory poems inspired by places, such as "Galway Bay" and the "Zennor Idyls." At the end of the volume are the "Epitaphs and Epigraphs," no doubt modeled after Blake but generally too trivial to be considered seriously on the level of poetry or philosophy: "The beautiful aeronaut and the butterfly/They get their wings, they copulate, and they die." Nevertheless, the range of Barker's talent is widening.

Within direct line of Barker's development are his triumphs of internalized expression, the "Bridal Nightmares," in which the subjective experience provides organic form. But the subjective approach comes to be balanced by the more direct style used in the poems on poets, in which Barker uses a sharp eye to capture the salient features of others and at the same time reveals himself. The failures of the volume result from the inconsistent mixture of the two styles. Although refinements in style become apparent when we look at the whole volume, it also contains some of his weaker poems. When he writes in the first person without a special audience, his strategy is sometimes inconsistent. When he writes to someone or about a particular person, as he does in ten

of the poems, the style is more direct; and the external controls
are obvious but not obtrusive. Significantly, only six of the thirty-
four poems are written from a detached view. When alienation is
treated on a cosmic scale, the poetry sometimes falters.

The poet writes, for example, the opening "Ode Against St. Cecilia's Day" in order to be able to face St. Cecilia's Day—to prepare for this "deserted anniversary." He laments the passing of a
traditional holiday which celebrated the patron saint of music and
hence harmony in the world. The title ironically reminds us of
Dryden's "Alexander's Feast" and of Pope's famous ode, both of
which celebrate a day when music reflected a social harmony
missing in the modern age.

The poem itself is dissonant. The elegiac tone is in tension with
Gothic or Surrealistic imagery and a midnight setting in which
abstractions come to life and nature is humanized. The extravagant rhetoric is unconvincing, for the poem urges the dead to
"Rise from the grave/Under a broken-hearted sky," then contra-
dicts itself by telling them to sleep, then asks somebody or something, presumably the dead, to stop our urge to kill—"the calling
killer in the skull." The hyperbole leads to meaningless inconsis-
tency. The speaker exhorts the dead to "hear the swansinging
nightmare," but then says that "Silence is her altar." He shouts to
no one in particular—the dead are dead and Cecilia is "in the
catacomb of her grandeur"; the "swansinging nightmares" dis-
solve into "the nightriding siren beautiful Caterwauling/War,"
hardly a griever for Cecilia's Day. Although war is a siren (in a
typical *double entendre*) in contrast to Cecilia, we are not adequately prepared for its appearance in the final stanza.

One of Barker's greatest temptations is the pathetic fallacy;
sometimes, as in the first poem of the title series, he lets personification get the better of the poem. The world, lost in the immen-
sity of space, is the "Cold shuttered star, skulker in clouds,/Street-
walker of the sky . . . ," the "outcast" of the universe. Like the
heroine of melodrama, she suffers because no one will take her in.
The news is that the world, searching for security, can "Never
come home."

The second "News of the World" does not communicate so directly. Peace is the abandoned mother and "wife of the workman
world," the poor housewife with a drunken husband and many
children who slaves over the "washing-board Time" though she is

sickly, "Coughing in fire and laurels." If we do not accept the indiscriminate mixture of allegory and symbol, we will assume that this poor female is dead from the start and hence incredible: her heart has been hatcheted and butchered. Although the "milky morning springs from her mothering breast," the sun, unlike milk, is no solace—it is "bitter" and keeps lions which the world will use for dismembering love, apparently synonymous with peace who is already dismembered. The sentimental implications, as well as the muddled allegory, can be attributed to the pathetic fallacy.

"News of the World III" presents similar problems. The world, this time personified as a sleeping woman like mother nature in the Golden Fleece elegy, is the wife of the speaker, who associates himself with mankind. The poem would be far more successful if the correspondence operated from individual experience outward; instead, it works from the amorphous, necessarily spiritual love of the world inward. It treats love of the world in terms of erotic connubial love. The emotional content is not convincing unless we take the symbol for the real content—unless we assume that this is a love poem from a man to his wife. Ultimately, the poem lacks fundamental unity of purpose and focus.

Thus the front page news is sometimes discouraging. Indiscriminate merging of the narrative of allegory with the connotative language of symbols, mishandling of the pathetic fallacy, and too much direct preachment (as in "The Five Faces of Pity") cause some poems to fall short of the remarkable standards of excellence established by others in *News of the World*.

IV   *The Demons of Negation*

A Vision of Beasts and Gods (1954) would be an appropriate title for all of the poetry Barker wrote during the 1950's. The eighteen poems are preoccupied with dualistic vision or with one or the other side of the dichotomy. Only four poems written since 1954 were included in the *Collected Poems* (1957), and the last of these—"Cycle of Six Lyrics"—manifests a continuing concern with antinomies. At least two titles in the series—"The Rose and the Rod" and "Heroes and Worms"—reveal the contraries. The dedication of *A Vision of Beasts and Gods* is indicative:

> Lean down, O loving hydra, out of the human
> Breast and persuade

> The ant to instruct us and the god to summon
> A guardian to our side.

Barker admits in effect what Dylan Thomas said with "I in my intricate image, stride on two levels." Barker, obsessed with the relationship between the two, tries in his early verse to deny the material level or to insist with Blake that spirit and flesh are one; the middle verse recognizes the separation of subject and object and of man and God; it nearly succumbs to despair over the corrupt, physical world and its reflection in the individual; and, in the 1950's, Barker is still plagued by the demons of negation.

"Sonnets of the Triple-headed Manichee" is a sequence dealing, as the title suggests, with intensified, demonic Manicheanism. In the *Collected Poems* the series has been placed with a group of sonnets from *News of the World* in order, it would seem, to imply that the poet has emerged from such terrifying negativism. The modern Manichee struggles with the despair concomitant with his acceptance of the separation of God from man. The spark of light that Manicheans identified with God and with the good is lost in the material world; it is completely beyond man's comprehension, although the spirits have instructed him regarding his dual nature. To the followers of this medieval heretical Christianity, the acceptance of the corruption of the physical universe may have been a satisfying explanation of man's state; but to the contemporary heretic, in a world where the intellect explains everything and nothing, the Manichean dualism is a source of dreadful doubt.

The first sonnet deals with the tormented search for the missing spirit and turns to modern man's anguished need for proofs:

> I was with that man when he rummaged his hand
> Among the guts of a god to fish for doves:
> The true wound chides that side without a wound
> For tendering nothing that attests or proves
> What telltale vision sleeps in a red hand.
> O from the wild and green hole of the human
> Heartful of lies and the forked tongues of grief,
> Let now the hooking claw of my doubt summon
> The glittering colossus of disbelief.
> I pitch through those receding zeroes of
> The doubt that, like recurring sevens, riddles

> The sum of all things. We are crucified
> Like serpents of the intellect on circles—
> O wounds, O crowns, O zeroes, bleed at my side.

The martyr is not Christ, but the man who has "rummaged his hand/Among the guts of a god to fish for doves." The god he seeks is simultaneously himself and the divine man; the agnostic rummages for God and, failing to find Him, searches himself. His side has no visible "wound," although he would prefer to have one; for nothing "attests or proves" the spark of spirit, the "Vision" that "sleeps in a red hand" of bestial man.

In accepting the fallen world as the only world, the speaker encounters nothingness, the circles and zeroes that are the Manichean martyr's crown. Like Blake's Urizen caught in the cycle of generation, Barker's reasonable man seems locked in a mathematical universe which reveals nothing of the absolute which he seeks. To him, the only absolute is the mathematician's zero or his receding sevens. The "wounds . . . crowns . . . zeroes" which crucify him are equivalent to the "receding zeroes of/The doubt that like recurring sevens" refutes the laws of probability. The circular crown of the martyr-to-mathematical fact is the cipher —the sum of things in an existence devoid of the "doves" of spirit.

In his late work Nietzsche, as the Antichrist, had tried to demonstrate the incompatability of a Christian and a scientific view of the world; and he had tried to set up his own god, Dionysus, in place of the crucified Christ. The second sonnet discloses that Nietzsche and those whose self-sufficiency tempts them to identify with him ironically crucify themselves. The man crucified with the speaker ("We are crucified . . .") is "Nietsche [*sic*] . . . martyred." The archetypal Dionysian suffers for his denial of God, whom he cannot find in nature or through reason. Although Nietzsche does not insist, as the Manichean would, that Satan created the visible world, he is tormented by his search for an eternal design. Barker's suggestion of Nietzsche's crucifixion is apt, for Zarathustra is in many ways similar to Christ; and, as Nietzsche's paranoic feelings of martyrdom grew he began, it seems, to identify with Christ.[12] Barker cites Nietzsche as evidence that man cannot live either without God or by making himself a god; he reveals himself as both disciple and critic of Nietzsche. He further

complicates the identification by asserting every man's involvement in the death of God.

The second sonnet controverts Sartre's atheistic Existentialism:

> Keelhauled across the starry death of God
> How loud I cry that hulk is truly shattered
> Showing the vascular burning ship and vessel
> In which the screaming Nietsche [*sic*] has been martyred.
> O lacerations multiply! O thousand tongues
> Affirm in the despairing hymns of blood
> That, like a right rolling among its wrongs,
> My God is dead, but his death can wrestle.
>
> What liberty we know among the stars
> No, is not liberty but a pillar to post
> Mopping and mowing of a cause that lost
> Its way and will boxing the compassed stars
> That now at half mast mourn over the vast
> Dead sea of the dead god of the dead stars.

The poem begins by asserting the wreckage of "I," Nietzsche, and
God. The speaker suffers, dragged under the keel of God's
wrecked hulk, which is "vascular" because the little vessel of biological man is contained within the burning ship. Man, who thinks
he is freed by God's death, has really gained only a semblance of
freedom—insignificant, unrewarding movement within the clichés
of existence which really lead nowhere—"a pillar to post/Mop-
ping and mowing." The stars, really part of the ship of God, are
also God's mourners—His flags "at halfmast" because His death
has destroyed the order of the universe and because its leader is
gone. The last lines, embodying the vast implications of the death,
repeat "dead" to hammer home its significance: the stars mourn
"over the vast/Dead sea of the dead god of the dead stars."

The final consequence of the death of God is the deification of
the "Siren of Negation" in Sonnet III:

> Answer me, answer me, Siren of negation!
> Whose face of mystery gazes from the mirror
> When we are out of the room? What voice
> Invokes a divine verb which we cannot hear?
> O globe that shatters at the exultation
> Of what we know we know. O perfect error

Proud in your pound of flesh, rejoice, rejoice:
Until this birth the unknown god slept here.

From the red worm inside a blind eye
She shall emerge in all her invisible splendour,
The vestal of negation, the sybil of absence,
And uttering the first anepiac cry
Shatter the categories of asserted grandeur
And to what is not delegate transcendence.

The siren is like Hecate, queen of the infernal regions: "As mother of death, dogs accompany her, as guardian of the door of Hades and as Goddess of dogs, she is of threefold form, and really identified with Cerberus."[13] Barker's triple-headed idol is the gate-keeper of the modern hell, the Manichean world which is the product of evil, a world in which we exalt "what we know we know."

The victory of evil in the contest with God is also the triumph of the mundane, egoistic man, who, like Shylock, is interested in the cruel letter of the law and in his own selfish gain. In exalting the world, man destroys the god in himself. The ugly symbol of man's lack of vision ("the red worm inside a blind eye") represents the emptiness of modern belief; the new goddess is guardian and prophetess of Existential nothingness. Her first inexpiable, sinless cry (for without God there is nothing to expiate and no sin) destroys the moral categories and the transcendental ideal. She deifies the known which, in fact, "is not"; for it represents the spiritual void of secular, scientific society.

"Sonnets of the Triple-headed Manichee" displays Barker's ability to organize and control his material to convey dread and anguish. The trilogy treats the individual martyrdom (I), its cause (II), and the effect of both (III). Although the imagery is tortured, each sonnet has a controlling symbol and each represents one of the heads of the monstrous Medusa of Manichean belief. Sonnet I focuses on the crucifixion of the agnostic; II, on God's death; and III, on the goddess of negation. The tension between what is and what should be is reflected in the contrast between subject matter and tone: the content denies transcendental values; the tone, agonized and ironic, affirms them. The poems communicate the horror of man without God and imply that, with Him, he would have freedom, mystery, and divine vision. The sonnets make up the most recent and perhaps the only poems in which Barker expresses such unmitigated metaphysical despair.

V   *Without Contraries is No Progression*

As if in answer to the awful negativism of Manicheanism, "Goodman Jacksin and the Angel" considers the problem of evil from another point of view. Unlike the sonnets which show the beast cut off from God, this poem envisions their interrelationship. Barker could have found ample precedent for his debate poem in medieval literature; he might also have found it in Yeats. The tetrameter lines suggest his late preference for the direct lyricism of Blake's songs and the late poetry of Yeats. The tone indicates the influence of Auden.

In a traditional debate between body and soul, each voice stands for a consistent set of ideas; in Barker's version, the attitudes shift and merge. The positions are indistinct, for both man and angel are questioning the nature of things. There is little real dissension, for the speakers illustrate the point of the dialectic— that contraries are essential to one another and in the end indistinct from one another. Barker writes finally that "At the living center of all this,/Evil and good, in expiation,/Dovetail the great antithesis." Barker's source books (Coleridge, Nietzsche, Blake, and Yeats) deal with the reconciliation of opposites. Barker marries heaven and hell, and he illustrates Blake's commandment— "Without contraries is no progression."

The dialogue begins with a flippant, cynical angel:

> Thus, Goodman Jacksin, time has come
> For truth in cockelshells and nuts;
> I beg you leave your head and home,
> Come, cut the cackle, (cackle cuts)
> And to the catchpenny cosmos show
> The vipers nuzzling in your guts
> And my tall spectres shaped of snow.

This masculine, Mephistophelean angel exhorts Jacksin to admit his dual nature. But even though his name proclaims his duality, Goodman Jacksin is at first complacent and skeptical. The angel argues, however, that the natural order in the world, "still your better half," is distorted. It's time to ask questions. Finally the

angel engages a reluctant Jacksin in argument by confronting him
with the Manichean dualism:

> What's it if this sanctuary,
> This holy of the holy heart
> Where, paraclete in an aviary,
> The mind beatifies every part
> That goes to make a singing soul—
> What's it to you if this bright temple
> Is split in two from pole to pole?
> Well, what's an earthquake, for example?

Kierkegaard described his own spiritual crisis as "The Great
Earthquake"; possibly Barker had been reading Kierkegaard or
Auden's presentation of him. Clearly, he had been reading Yeats.

The angel is thinking of the spiritual value of art, the sanctuary
of permanence Yeats created in "Sailing to Byzantium." Barker is
not writing about *any* Jacksin; he is writing about the Romantic
poet. The mind, like Yeats' "sages standing in God's holy fire," is
the intercessor; Barker's "singing soul" is an oblique reference to
Yeats' "singing-masters of my soul." Even the aviary is borrowed
from "Sailing to Byzantium" where the birds in the trees symbolize the dying generations and the golden bird, the eternity of art,
which transcends the conflicts of the world of birth and dying.
The angel's question regarding the complete cleavage between
the thing and its essence reminds us, however, of Yeats' conclusion
to "Among School Children"—"How can we know the dancer
from the dance?"

When Jacksin answers the angel, he insists that after all man is,
as Yeats put it in "The Circus Animals' Desertion," "fastened to a
dying animal." Jacksin recognizes his kinship with the world of
Becoming:

> With these bright eyes I have witnessed
> What the bright ploughshare also sees;
> The running generations harnessed
> In green laws to divine decrees:
> The seeding generations under
> Every winter solstice stir,
> And, from the earth at a dead end,
> A daughter rise up, praising her.

The angel, the devil's advocate and perhaps the Yeats of the Byzantium poems, mocks the "curious privilege of dirt":

> You lay
> Your rag and bone down in a grave
> To fructify dirt in a way—
> But this is all the part you have.

The "rag and bone" alludes to the last stanza of "The Circus Animals' Desertion" in which Yeats asserts that everything has its beginning in the "foul rag and bone shop of the heart" and that
antinomies produce one another. The beautiful needs the ugly;
the mind, the body. This Yeatsian idea is the key to Barker's poem.

The speakers argue over whether we are all rag and bone or
whether we can ascend to "greater purposes." Since man is always
"axing oracles with a fact," why should he expect "heavenly vision?" Jacksin argues that there is a "husband jack" to whom he is
related and, by implication, whose vision he should share. The
angel sees this creator as "a fiend," (as Barker saw Him in "Sacred
Elegy V") instead of a friend. In life, the manifestations of the
demon are sexual. Perhaps Satan (or Pan) is the god of this world:
"The rooftops bear his sinning track./His goat hooves outrage
bed and birth!"

Jacksin gets at the core of the enigma, however, with "You rave
like any soapbox gabber,/Evil is simply this my friend:/A good
we do not understand." The man is reminded of original sin (and
probably of the issues of *Paradise Lost*), for he sadly admits that
he is the son of Adam and hence of

> An old man whom I cannot see,
> A fathering farmer of farrows,
> With his blackjack spade, a gun on his knee,
> And his everlasting quarrels:—

The feuding, irritable, anthropomorphic father is a God no better
than Nobodaddy. *Paradise Lost* looms in the background when
Barker continues,

> Jehovah also saw you stride
> Out of a green and guarded gate
> Into the mystery of your fate:

. . . .
> As, tracking, anxious, secret, saw
> The hounds of hell rout out and start
> All the sorrow you were born for.

Echoing Hopkins' "Spring and Fall"—the plight "man was born for"—Jacksin recognizes his responsibility to pursue the truth of the enigma of evil: "Obvious Evil, as it seems,/Emerges, in a little while,/Redeemed, and white, and provident." It is hard, however, to accept the dialectical relationship as just: "The laws of act and consequence/Obey a justice none/May follow with a rational sense—"

To illustrate the irrationality of the universe Jacksin and the angel range over the mysteries of beauty and ugliness and reveal that opposites can come from one another. The angel asserts that sex is evil, and yet the product, "the innocent image," is good. Barker is surely thinking of Yeats' "Leda and the Swan" when he writes that the spiritual may engender the material thing, "The falling feather can engender. . . . A generation of clashing rocks": "And conceptions of great spiritual splendour/Derive, through successions of paradox,/From brief moments of cheap misery."

The mystery proves too much for the angel, who admits that he too is a "dog's demigod" and that he pities man for his inheritance of "The property of error." Jacksin retorts sardonically, "which of us, in truth/Could ever really forgive the other?/And who could ever forgive us both?" Both questioners are guilty, for both lack humility. The angel says that God demands idolatry, and blind adoration apparently reminds Jacksin-Barker of Kierkegaard's study of Abraham in *Fear and Trembling:*

> And yet what can we do if we are
> Swept up in such a storm of wings
> As that authoritative power—
> What do save cower in our fear?
> Then in that bosomed and huge cave
> Crouch, trusting that our cooing love
> Declare in fear and tremblings:
> We are crushed out by that thunder?

The act of faith in God's elect is not so vivid to Jacksin as is the fear of an angry God, who's more the God of Apocalypse than Kierkegaard's God of Love; perhaps Jacksin has paid too little attention to worshipping God. He has loved "all living things" instead of "the landlord of the infinite." Love itself is, as it was in some of the earlier poems, the good maternal Eros whom "All living things obey."

Thus Barker presents the thesis and antithesis of another conundrum. Love, the creative principle, and God, the wrathful Jehovah, provide the dialectic of existence:

> In the arched dialectic by
> Which all existence must evolve,
> There is no wallflower at the dance,
> On all things that first law devolves.
> And thus the innocent must die
> Because its very innocence
> By law of opposition calls
> The skulls to lead it in that dance.

The law of opposition in the dance-macabre of life is the only answer Barker can find in the law of change that dominates physical existence.

In an allegory that calls to mind both Milton and Blake, he describes the opposites of creation and destruction: "Love and Death" combined and "Then from their open-eyed embrace/Rose the first god that ever was,/With doom in his face." That first god, the god-man, is subject to the laws of generation. Perhaps reconciled to existence but reminded of mortal man's insignificance, Jacksin suddenly cries, *O vanitas vanitas;* his body is no more than grass; his soul, a mere flickering flame:

> How shall I speak of mystery
> With a gun and a pound in my hand?
> I must obey a master I
> Shall never understand.
> All flesh is grass, all grass is flesh
> And the midnight sun roars down:
> I and my soul go up in a flash,
> I and my soul go down.

The conclusion reiterates the dialectic, but the law of process is not comforting since ultimately Jacksin and his angel "go down." Barker's answer to the enigma of existence is poetic, not philosophical. He does not present a system, but his ideas derive primarily from Yeats, who might well be the journeyman-Jacksin speaker. Barker's argument is not so clear as to insist that the synthesis in this clash and combination of opposites will always be a higher form; but, in calling it "the arched dialectic," he reminds us faintly of Yeats' conical gyres. Barker presents evidence for the emotional acceptance of the idea that opposites are essential; that they attract; and, as "The law of dialectics" in love proves, they finally become one. "Goodman Jacksin and the Angel" is the only later poem that sets for itself the task of transcending contraries. It prepares the way for the Dionysian acceptance which becomes a major theme in the poems of the 1950's.

VI   *The Dionysian Muse*

In "Consolatory Verses for the Middle Years," Barker alleges that the poet celebrates the communion of creatures. The speaker interprets the end of winter as an affirmation of life, "of beast, idea, and stone." With less vitality and intensity than Shelley, who wrote "Be thou, Spirit fierce, My spirit," the modern Romantic seeks inspiration in the sacred lyre of the wind. Although the youthful fire is missing, the constituents of the Romantic attitude are proclaimed. Like Yeats, Barker affirms the transcendent, the holy poem, and the vision of tragic beauty; the creative process is painful, the imaginary perception torn out of the mind. He dedicates to Pythia, priestess of Apollo, the Apollonian muse, "The no longer easy/Paean and praise of a heavier heart and hour." He honors the oracular power of poetry and the courageous acceptance of life. He insists that "tall men walk upright in lightning because/It calls for more courage." The "Ode to the West Wind" makes a good companion piece for Barker's poem, but Shelley's ecstasy has become in Barker a middle-aged sigh.

"Letter to a Young Poet" labels Barker's poetry. For the yea-sayer, "every No that sense could express/Turned to a transcendental Yes." Dionysian art affirms life in spite of its inherent dissonance and change. The poet must inscribe a positive upon the negative of life; for, in art, thesis and antithesis make a synthesis. The symbol-making visionary poet sees objects of the external world as symbols of the internal life. "All enigmas/Describe themselves in terms of stars":

> There is a spirit of turbulence
> Inhabiting the intelligence

> Determined always to impose
> Another reason on the rose
>
> Another cause upon the creature
> Than the privilege of its nature;
> A handcuff and a history
> Upon all natural mystery
>
> And this turbulent spirit starts
> That insurrection in our hearts
> By which the laws of poetry
> Are broken into anarchy:
>
> The anarchy that seeks to show
> An altitude which way to go,
> Or use astronomy to prove
> That duty is our only love.

The spirit of turbulence is the Dionysian muse, the tumultuous inspiration which defies the rules to set up its own system; but its instrument is the imagination which synthesizes opposites like astronomy and duty. Implicit in this view is an exalted concept of the poet as creator. The poem itself is a solace, like a mother hen, Hopkins' Holy Ghost, or Barker's mother world; for it "folds its wings/And from a bloody breast will give/Even to those who disbelieve." As Auden did in the third section of "In Memory of W. B. Yeats," Barker uses a poem to another poet to define the function of poetry; like Auden, he chooses tetrameter quatrains to assert that the poem itself is a kind of absolute. Writing it or appreciating it is in itself an assent to life, but science and reason are always prepared to destroy the consolations of imagination:

> By the known world the intellect
> Stands with its bright gun erect,
> But the long loving verities
> Are kissing at the lattices.

Despite the Romantic assertion of distrust of the intellect and of faith that transcendental verities become one, Barker's dark Dionysian voices remind him that "we do not know what is."

Dylan Thomas was a poet who said yes to life. It is not, therefore, surprising that "At the Wake of Dylan Thomas" apostrophizes the Welsh poet with "O Dionysian." Thomas' outstanding quality is, to Barker, his ability to make poems "simply from joy" and to summon up the world of childhood, as he did in *In Country Sleep* and *A Child's Christmas in Wales*. Thomas is the voice of a world of "wise-eyed infants/Whose innocence has survived all living onslaughts": "That cloudy boy harping among the graves/Will lead a doxological choir of loves./O the dirt sings because all joy is magical." Barker is especially aware of his fellow Romantic's affirmation of life. The "one undoubting Thomas" is an appropriate pun which fits the exuberant vitality of this elegy for "the master of the house" of words, who could hide "All his knowledge in the vessel/Of a divine and a divining image."

The elegy makes Thomas' death a victory. In another poem commemorating the death of a contemporary, Barker again makes death a triumph. "The Death of Manolete," one of the most interesting, although seemingly most difficult, poems in the volume, seeks to immortalize a bullfighter. Like a T. S. Eliot poem, this poem illustrates the pastness of the past and its presence, as well as the relation of archetypes of rebirth to individual and contemporary experience. Barker uses in conjunction with references to the actual death of Manolete, others to the legend of Mithra, the sun-god deity of truth and light who struggled with a great bull that allegorically represented the powers of evil. In the legend, Mithra, by slaying the bull and by letting its blood, symbolically fructified the earth; similarities to vegetation rites are clear. The soul of the Sacred Bull became guardian of birds and flocks, and Mithra became the creator of life. In Mithraic liturgy, on Black Friday, the taurobolium or bull-slaying was presented. Mithra, worn out by battle was depicted in a stone image on a bier as a corpse. He was mourned and then, after three days in a tomb, removed in great rejoicing.

Reference to the taurobolium forms the background for the poem:

> You, king, die. Mithra. Where was death
> Hiding for those ten hours when you lay
> Endowing Lenares with that great red legend?
> The Monster. Dead. Drag the bright corpse away.
>
> Did the sword shriek in his hand? The sand
> Wept as he fell. You, king, die. The Miura
> Groaned as he gored his god. But the long
> Face of a stone and a saint only set surer

Into the calm that had always crowned it. You,
King, die. The killer with a bull's hair on his belly
Goes towering to his death under a cape.
Black that Islero honours the place where he fell.

O expiation! The king and the bull, kissing,
Enter and share a kingdom. The sword and horn
Sleep side by side. Justice. You, kings die.
Between this man and this bull a myth is born.

In juxtaposing an archetypal myth and a real, contemporary event, Barker gives both meaning. The bullfighter, in a sense acting the role of Mithra, really dies. In rëenacting the legend, he becomes one with it, transmuted into art. In goring his god, the bull too is subsumed in legend.

The first stanza presents in quick, stabbing phrases and sentences the actual fact; the second makes it clear, however, that Barker is thinking of the stone statue representing the death scene; the third indicates that the animal (representing the material world and evil) in killing the god-man achieves great stature: he "goes towering to his death" and it is "Black," not simply because it is, in terms of the myth, Black Friday, but because the town of Islero "honours the place where he fell." The inhabitants of the Spanish town—and, by extension, of the modern world—honor the "king and bull" together.

If Manolete-Mithra and the bull represent good and evil, this poem is another assertion that opposites become one. The beast and the god, the animal and the man become one in death and achieve continued life through legend and art. The animal is the substance; the man, the form of creation. Until the modern age, the sun-god hero of spirit defeated the material universe; but now the poet affirms life, even if it is a black day when the material substance is elevated to equal importance with the spiritual form. Barker forges a myth to assert his acceptance of the importance of physical life. The antitheses are synthesized, and their story makes a new mythology. Even the pathetic fallacy, "The sand/Wept as he fell" is justifiable when we realize that Mithra was not supposed to die; the bull who was to fructify the sand has, in doing so, destroyed the god. By the end of the poem, the bull has achieved status equal with the king's, so that the terse refrain

"You, king, die," becomes "you, kings, die." The opposites are united in death, and the bull has been deified. The poet has indeed come to accept life.

VII   *Manfred Pursued by Furies*

Barker's affirmations are always tempered by negations, for Wordsworth's joy does not inspire him so easily as Byron's melancholy. Several lyrics in *A Vision of Beasts and Gods* are the bad dreams of a guilty lover, and in "The Mnemonic Demigod" the inferior deity of memory haunts him with ghosts of the past. The constituents are Byronic: The solitary persona muses in a natural setting upon his past and the victims and victors of love. Nature serves, however, rather to accuse Barker than to give him the solace it gave Manfred or Childe Harold. Standing by the house where he once lived, the speaker muses,

> This stream
> By which my old house stands
> Like a water of faces
> Speaks and accuses me
> With a perpetual wringing of wrongs.

A similar theme informs the nightmare poems called "Justice at Midnight." The wild children in "The Ballad of Wild Children" are demons of what the speaker did. He dreams of a raging storm in which he is pursued by these children "My heart disowns . /O orphans of all blind egoes" of "the eagle/Or vulture I am—." Although the "huge gears" of the Newtonian universe "grind up all power and all glory," the children of the past return "howling out loud/For Justice and Vengeance,/While, overhead smiling, blood drips from the jaws/Of the heavenly engines."

After the sweeping movement of the "Ballad of the Wild Children," the title poem, "Justice at Midnight," quietly controlled in tetrameter quatrains, treats a midnight interview with Justice, who is personified as a woman who examines the speaker's conscience and his "Impenitential violence." He remembers his sins, his "dead brides," and "seven more to keep," the wild children. When Justice comes, the world ends; for the only justice fit for his crimes, says the breast-beating Romantic, is death. In "The Caterwauling Beast at Last Has Utterance," the third poem of the series, the salacious male, full of self-recrimination, bewails his beastial, guilty nature with an ironic prayer to the "Dove, whom I never knew and shall never know."

Barker's philanderer also speaks in later poems. When "A Domestic Poem" appeared in *Poetry Magazine*,[14] it was notable for its musical, controlled economy and for the consistency of its Freudian symbols. The poem was, however, extended in the *Collected Poems;* in it, the self-contained lyric is related to the archetypal pattern. The husband and wife become Adam and Eve; the unfaithful husband is the "vindictive Adam" who "Avenges a lost Eden." The indictment of love and marriage is perhaps less effective in its final form than it was when Barker was content with the individual experience which reflects, without insisting upon, the universal. The poem explores the dual feelings of the unfulfilled, forsaken wife and of the husband who wishes to escape her. The "Monologue of the Wife" expresses the female desire that the male "aggrandize my furrow/And glorify what's born." The "Monologue of the Husband" expresses the male animal's desire for escape from the yoke of marriage. She is the fallow field; he, the harrower. The "beast devouring flesh/Is jaded of its own." The sated philanderer, full of self-disgust, ends the poem declaring:

> No love, no love, no love,
> O let no brightness in—
> But the sheet-lightning shove
> Where we end, and begin.

The final cycle of lyrics in *Collected Poems* exemplifies the style and subject matter of Barker in the late 1950's. Still struggling with personal polarities, he wishes for the doves of spirit to "dismember me" (I); he recognizes Christ's dual nature, "the rose and the rod," the love and the fiery purgation (II); he loves the "pearl and breasted world" (V) and wishes to be not Narcissus but the star—to look at the "sweet star" rather than the infernal "hot pit" of self, so that he can find "Glory without regret/For all things ever after" (VI). The dualistic war has taken on a distinctly Christian framework. The struggle is epitomized in the lyric "Heroes and Worms" (III). The beast and the angel are evident:

The dragons of the breast
Devour and drag down
Those seraphim of the mind
Trumpeting to attest
That Destiny is our own.
But what is not is best.

I, cowboy with a spear,
Transfix my own heart
To kill the worm down there
Tearing St. George apart—
But O the worm turns
Into my heart of hearts.

The speaker cannot defeat the heart's passions, which destroy the idealist in him and cause self-torment. Barker skillfully reveals the struggle between the aspiring knight of holiness and the dragons of passion. The important words of the first stanza are deflated in the second: the hero is only a cowboy; and his dragon, St. George's fiery antagonist, is only the sexual worm. "Heroes and Worms" exemplifies Barker's mature lyricism in its directness, lucidity, and carefully restrained music; it juxtaposes to unresolved tension the security of form.

VIII   *Directions in Form and Content*

Although the "Justice at Midnight" series develops in line with Barker's poems of internalized expression, in later work Barker is increasingly objective. His poems gain concreteness and detachment when he focuses on a specific event. In the slight, but successful "On a Friend's Escape from Drowning," he treats the potentially sentimental subject of a wife's saving her husband from drowning as their child looks on. By carefully keeping outside of the picture, the poet communicates the pathos of the event. One of his most objective poems, it significantly celebrates the preservation of life. Among other poems which reveal increased control in relation to narrowing subject matter are those occasioned by his travels—meditations in Italy "At the Tombs of the Medicis" and "Stanzas on a Visit to Longleat House in Wiltshire, October, 1953." Although there are lapses in control, caused usually by the insurgent pathetic fallacy, as in the "Epitaph for Many Young Men," Barker becomes, on the whole, very sure of himself. His syntax becomes direct, his meter measured. The last lyrics in *Collected Poems,* carefully set lyrical gems, indicate his growing preference for clarity and control.

The most characteristic theme of *A Vision of Beasts and Gods* and the cycle of lyrics in *Collected Poems* is the struggle with religious feeling. But even as Barker jousts with holiness, the worm wins out. The poetry comes from the conflict between self and selfish desires and the religion he would like to accept. Two recent plays, *The Seraphina* and *In the Shade of the Old Apple Tree*[15] attest to Barker's religious quest and to his need, sometimes ironic, sometimes flagellant, to accept an impossible God whom he loves. His need for belief seems to derive from his double awareness of his power and weakness, of the hero and the worm.

In the "Ballad of the Muse at Sea" the speaker, sensing a loss of power, bitterly fears his inspiration is waning. The muse, or poet, is perplexed and uncertain because he desires divine afflatus and finds only bitter memories of former strength. He misses the bird of inspiration and now sees only "the fallen feathers" of "the seabird of desire/Turned into bitter salt." Nostalgically, he looks back to his early power:

> The mounted dolphins of my heart
>   Sprang up the fiery stairs
> Into the sunrise. And never to part
>   Joy went about in pairs.
>
> I felt the mind in a great deep
>   Roll like a whale possessed
> Across the breeding ground of my sleep
>   And break out of my breast.
>
> . . . .
>
> So lofty over rock and bar
>   The young rainbow hung
> I held all hazardous things that are
>   Under the arch of my tongue.
>
> Asleep in tempests of the mind
>   Such halcyons lay smiling
> That every affliction seemed to find
>   A pearl of reconciling.

The best poems of the 1950's are, indeed, pearls which reconcile negatives of affliction.

CHAPTER 7

The Sixties:
Solaces and Satires

DESPITE a paradoxical title which suggests whistling in the
dark, *The View from a Blind I* (1962) contains none of the
awful questioning and less of the guilt and disillusionment of former volumes. The "blind eye" refers to the secularism of the third
sonnet "of the Triple-headed Manichee." The title implies what
the poems corroborate—that they are often occasioned by places
and the poet's attitudes toward them. The poet in exile attests to
the triumph of the world's beauty over the defiled heart of man.
Poems for people are affectionate or admiring; but annoyance
with places, people, and movements is etched in satire. His views
of Italy are largely favorable, but his picture of America is bit-
ingly critical. He associates Italy with natural and traditional
values and America with an unnatural break with tradition.

I *Nothing to Loathe in Nature*

The series called "Roman Poems" discloses the influence of
nature and the new calm. "Roman Poem 1" evokes a picture, mood,
and the absolving ascendancy of the scene on the "Jaded nature"
of the speaker. It recommends "spiritual expiation" by the water,
through immersion in love of the elemental world. In "Roman
Poem 2," the description of a shower in Rome reminds the speaker
of impending death; but, as the shower ends, radiance breaks
everywhere except in his heart, until he forgets, for the moment,
his "blinding sheets" and feels "the spirit dance"; "human delight"
almost restores hope.

"Roman Poem 3" is less idyllic. In what amounts to a prose
account, the persona describes hanging artificial birds in an empty
birdcage and listening to the sad music the wind made in them,
music like threnodies "torn from a falling harp. . . ." "The children fed them with flowers"; the wind dismantled them. Then one

151

morning a wounded sparrow appeared; the children tried to help him, but there among the artificial birds, "its monstrous Idols, the little bird died. And, for my part,/I hope the whole unimportant affair is/quickly forgotten. The analogies are too trite." And so Barker resists the temptation to speak of man's dark destiny and his false gods and, more specifically, of the poet's fate and his art, as well as of the artists whom he reveres. The analogy to Yeats' contrast between the artificial and real birds in *Sailing to Byzantium* may indeed seem to the jaded exile something of a cliché. The poet is devoted to the artificial music, the artifact, the imitation of reality; but he himself, having suffered the slings and arrows of time, is like the real bird come to an aviary of art—Rome —to die. The language of flat statement and the refusal to draw a moral help to justify the straightforward *vers libre,* itself appropriate to the dominant world-weary attitude. The poet, like the insignificant sparrow, ineffectual among his "idols," is ready somehow to make his peace, "like a lost soul electing to die in Rome."

"A Little Song in Assisi" is reminiscent of the first Roman poem. The spirit of the gentle St. Francis is reflected in this appreciation of beauty. "Variations on Swans" again treats the visual effect of a scene on the poet. Variation I is filled with quiet reverence for natural beauty, but Variation II is not so assured. The speaker wishes to be "with the wild swan," that noble part of himself that is gone. The *ubi sunt* motif is clear: the waters move on; the swan glides away. Barker communicates the sense of loss in something of a swan song for the birds of spirit, beauty, and imagination that inspired Yeats' "The Wild Swans at Coole."

As the mind of the modern Romantic goes to work on the objective world, it projects the poet's own sense of emptiness, his fear that his poetic vision is failing. The title poem sets up a central dichotomy: the view is "void" because the speaker's "eye . . . [is] blind." He blames himself for not seeing that nature is good: "Farms so fecund, so genial/With their windfalling gifts/Of what is at heart so wholly/Given to all that is good." He chides himself for reading his own faults "into Eden"; nature is, he asserts, liberal and charitable:

> Do fountains hesitate
> To offer their perpetual
> And charitable oblations?

The olive is liberal over
Her husbanding generations.

But the evidences of man's degraded spirit are also there—"the
broken Imperial pillar" reminds him of man's stony heart. In a
country whose history and religion modern man inherits, nature is,
nevertheless, generous, and out of the antinomies—eros and
thanatos, innocence and experience—will arise the symbols of
new life. The poem ends the volume on a positive note of acceptance.

The positive note also informs poems for people. "Poem as Dedication" reveals the poet's commitment to friends and loved ones
who wander now in his memory, separated from him by "the sea/
or the wide grave, or time." In "2 Poems for Painters," which actually appeared first in *London Magazine* in February, 1956, Barker
lauds Kit Barker and Francis Bacon for creating beauty out of
anguish. The nightmarish imagery and the tragedy of artistic
suffering that Barker interprets in them belong to an earlier mode
of Barker's verse, but the two poems also mirror the appreciative
mode of the 1962 volume. Kit Barker's heroic efforts to paint,
"trapped among catastrophies," make him a Perseus "hounded by
Medusa down." Barker cannot forget the disaster of his brother's
"sacrificed eye," a sacrifice for which he still feels guilt. Kit Barker,
like Francis Bacon, who paints with a "wronged hand" "The flood-
light of human agony," is among the tragic artists who wear the
"heavy crown."

In line with the poems dedicated to other artists is an "Elegy for
David Gray, 1838–1860," an insignificant nineteenth-century suicide whose ardour, dedication, and suffering Barker understands.
He quotes Matthew Arnold as an epigraph: "David Gray—the
temperament, the talent itself, is deeply influenced by their mysterious malady; the temperament is *devouring;* it uses vital power
too hard and too fast. . . ." The aging Barker, himself once con-
sumed by passionate artistic aspirations, can emphathize with the
agonies and privations of a personality among those who "Bar-
tered their lives for the immortal feather" of poetic achievement.

Assuaging appreciation never extends to the "I" of the poems.
The mood of self-recrimination, perhaps the most persistent in all
of Barker's poetry, informs several poems. "I Walked by a Win-
dow in Ireland" reminds him of his "sinnermost heart." He de-

scribes walking on Christmas Eve in Dublin with a friend, no doubt Patrick Swift to whom the poem is dedicated, but whose name suggests the saint who brought Christianity to Ireland and the Dean of Dublin who satirized man for his lack of the Christian virtues he espoused. Patrick Swift is, by implication, a Christ who knocks on the door of Christian hearts and is not allowed to enter. Ironically, in Catholic Ireland on the night that should celebrate the gift of giving and the gift of Love, the poet and his friend are not "listened to, nor loved. . . ." But one must give to receive, and "never a loving word/Have we ever really heard/or ever spoken." The poet indicts himself and all mankind for lacking charity.

In the mournful night ballad, "True love, True Love, what have I done?" the restless, tormented persona thinks of his responsibility in destroying love; he has seen love and beauty depart, martyred; and he himself drowns "In assuaging sea," haunted by love. In the same vein, "The Maidenhair Vessel with the Cradling Chain," written in octaves with alternating rimes (*ababab*), laments the loss of a lovely hyacinth girl whose "innocence of spirit" the speaker has destroyed. The title suggests obliquely that she has suffered loss of maidenhead as well as possible impregnation. His milkmaid love, "her hair tossed and tawny . . . traipsing down the evening/Track," has fled. And still the Byronic lover, a Satan beguiling Eve, blames himself for her going—for stepping "from behind a bush" and seducing her. He blames himself for loving too much and regrets that "innocence must either alter or die." Yet, although there is a world between them, in his mind "They marry at the middle star." The guilty lover is not, as in former poems, the unmitigated fatal male, nor is the girl simply the blighted rose. No longer as vain as he says he is, he recognizes that the girl had courage to leave him. He suffers for violating her and for losing this innocent "dove."

"The Fiery Beds of Flesh" contains no innocent dove, only the "fingering worm" ever-present in the bed of sensual lovers "Underneath their tolling death"; the carefully wrought poem is full of the sound and fury of infernal sex practiced in defiance and despair of imminent death:

> 'Yet here, instead, at this hot bed
> I feel the third cold hand

> At my breast laid, here at my heart
> I feel the third cold hand.'
>
> They gazed with carrion eyes, and sighs
> Across the fiery bed
> But like a prize that snake-head shone
> Across the fiery bed.

In contrast to the nature and love poems is the mocking satiric verse. The major target of Barker's poisoned arrows is the United States. "Circular from America" begins as a doggeral denunciation of the Beat Movement, but the critic, carried away by his skill with lethal weapons, strikes at almost everything American. Despite its extravagance, the indictment is more effective than that of the early American Odes. Its slapdash dimeter and pointed puns hit the mark, as when Jack Kerouac, for example, is ridiculed for his paucity of ideas:

> But ½ an idea
> To a hundred pages
> Now Jack, dear Jack,
> That ain't fair wages
> For labouring through
> Prose that takes ages
> Just to announce
> That Gods and Men
> Ought to study
> The Book of Zen.

Barker aims also at Gregory Corso, Kenneth Rexroth, William Carlos Williams, and Greenwich Village artists for whom

> O its early to bed
> You story tellers
> If you're not on Fulbrights
> Or Rockefellers.

After he makes fun of the language and sexual habits of the Beat, he broadens the indictment "From Maine to Utah . . . On the other side/Of the Middle Worst. . . ." And in New York City everyone is, according to Barker, dreaming of being someone else or going to an analyst. He insists that the ghost of a great "Demo-

cratic conception/Shrieks out: 'I confess/To a little deception.
. . .'" American values, "The pyrotechnics/Of shall I say Hell/
Have reached Minneapolis/And St. Paul as well."

In Colorado, Barker is even more disillusioned; the "9 Beati-
tudes to Denver," are written in a long-line sprung rhythm (usually with five stresses to a line) which facilitates a prosaic style
that moves readily from the bombastic to the banal. The first Beatitude (and, of course, the title is an ironic pun) is a mock prayer
for preservation from the outward signs of middle-class values. It
protests to the secular God of American mass culture against the
"drums of middle class regiments and the Pegasi of Mobilgas."
The second Beatitude, which criticizes science's dehumanizing
effects, attacks modern man for making himself the object of the
"Bureau of Psychological Statistics"—an engine without heroism
or understanding of past heroism. One step beyond Nietzsche's
proclamation of the death of God and hence of old values, Barker
ironically questions "when the heroic machine weeps at Thermop-
ylae/Why does it mourn? The great god, man, is dead."

Beatitude III proceeds from the assumption that man in America is a machine dominated by technology and science, to speak of
sex as dehumanized and sterile. At the same time, it attacks man's
efforts to reach the moon as no more than a sexual assault. Like a
Swift in Laputa, Barker twits man's presumptuous pride in science. The fourth Beatitude asserts in still another way Barker's disapproval of American attitudes—"the essential cynicism/Of a society invented by beach boys and supported by girls without
girdles." Instead of the stations of the cross, he finds only "The
Fourteen Stations of the Beatitude to Denver" and wonders
whether we should "crucify Rexroth [Kenneth Rexroth], and
force him to be a god?"

Still another beatitude (V) mocks the American female, the hip
courtesan, in tones of overstated compliment: "when I mislaid my
female in Memphis/How could I ever have known such a Thais
would succeed her?" He denigrates her by praising her irresistible
record collection, her horse-tail hair, and her sexual athleticism;
then he undercuts the exaggerated praise of the incongruous and
inconsequential by suggesting her essential inhumanity with "I
kiss your mouth like a gas ring." The speaker's self-contempt is, of
course, implicit in his attack on the empty promiscuity of a
woman he is willing to use for sexual gratification.

In attacking Beat high-seriousness and shallow pretentions, Barker insists that the pronouncement "whose central proposition is, simply, to love" is an excuse just to go "to pot together in the name of man." The pun on "pot" is as much a part of his indictment as the punning in "It is better to lie together than to tell the truth apart." Sexual freedom without responsibility is simply a form of escape. Beatitude VIII, addressed to Walter Ruether, the antithesis of all that is "beat," asserts, indeed, that the core of Beat vacuity lies in social irresponsibility. Emancipated moderns, lauding the moral quietism of their cult, are "The cherubim of the present . . . trumpeting on a cloud/Of laotzean tea"—or so they think. Barker, disgusted with rejection of traditional Western values, undercuts angelic references with "Where the hell is the roadmap to Pandemonium?" He disdains the refusal to listen to "the boring dead" and despises their preference for the antic and absurd: "No, let us go to the park and hear what the chairs are saying."

Allen Ginsberg is the only guru whom Barker can admire, for Ginsberg is a prophet of the breakdown of American values; in capturing the fragmentation of reality he "Howled" and showed "her disconsolate heart. It is much to his honour that he has not attempted/To edit her real hysteria. Or his own" (IX). Most important to Barker is the awareness—an awareness that he thinks Beats tried to disavow—that "The consequences of what we have done still wear mourning." His universe is inescapably moral. No wonder then, that life among the Beats is not blessed. It is, as Barker mockingly presents it, a round of marijuana; bacchanals; mechanical, irresponsible, often perverse sex; a pretentious interest in Oriental philosophy; a refusal of the lessons of the past; and a failure to face present reality, the reality of moral responsibility.

Barker's scorn of modern modes of hypocrisy does not stop with the bohemian avant-garde of the 1950's. Still in the satiric vein Barker lashes out against the literary pretentions of the Scotch in "Scottish Bards and an English Reviewer." Inviting comparison to Byron's "English Bards and Scotch Reviewers," Barker is as extravagant and indiscriminate in his attack as Byron was. But, where Byron took revenge on critics as well as English bards and would-be bards, Barker directs his arrows at the Scotch. An occasional poem describing the talk in a Scotch pub, it needles Scotsmen who think themselves misunderstood and underrated—the

greatest poets alive " 'Now Dylan's dead. . . ." Barker strikes the
"chip" they wear on their shoulders and their "strutting" drunken
pride in poetry promised but not written:

> Canna ye see
> We're marvellous?
> Without so much as
> One word written
> We're the finest poets
> In all Britain.
> Stand me a pint
> O the singing stuff
> An' I'll shoot ye an epic straight
> Off me cuff.

The "Scottish Bards and an English Reviewer" epitomizes Barker's late bent for witty ridicule, the amused sneer, the satiric grin;
for direct colloquial speech, blunt, bawdy, impatient, rough, and
masculine. Except for its two stress lines, it is written in a style
like that of *The True Confession of George Barker*.

The extremes in style in *The View from a Blind I* are the witty
satires and the idyllic lyrics. The volume is notable because the
poet is less preoccupied with himself than usual. The satiric
poems direct his spleen at others; the nature poems focus on the
world outside him or on the solace natural beauty provides for the
world-weary poet who regrets approaching age and waning
powers. He could write with a fellow world traveler, Byron's
Childe Harold, that he "can see/Nothing to loathe in nature"; for
the trouble stems from human nature. He is annoyed but not out-
raged by that "mouth of an ass the heart." Barker is, for all his
cynicism, mellowing. In a way, *The View from a Blind I* represents a near triumph for the external—the world of places and
people to which the poet, suspicious of subjective self-dramatiza-
tion, directs his muse. A new depth, a new calm, a new humility
balance the brash, barbed criticism of a poet provoked by vanity
and vulgarity into satiric defense of an essentially Christian hu-
manism.

II   *The Heart Laid Bare*

The True Confession of George Barker: I & II (1964) reveals
the double man torn between belief and behavior, theism and

naturalism. This cynical autobiography, Book I of which appeared in 1950 and became the first half of the 1964 edition, is informed by the same stanza and by much the same tone and material as François Villon's *Testaments*. While Villon is alternately mischievous and scarifying, Barker's mischief is largely linguistic—he gives full range to his delight in punning and word play; he combines elements of bitter-sweet melancholy and sardonic self-recrimination. These reactions rise out of the conflict, in Book I, between self-pity and self-disgust and, in Book II, between an apparently obsessive need for God and a correlative sense of alienation. When not directed at God, the irony turns inward on self.

Barker clearly indicates his debt to "that Frenchman" for stanzaic form, intention (to "catalogue/Every exaggerated human claim") and personal similarity ("No, not the magnitude . . . but the type's the same."). Villon's rebel Catholicism, his vilification of enemies, his insistence that everything ends in wenches and taverns, and his frank treatment of forbidden subject matter are precedents for the modern poem.

The self-revelation of the confession is, of course, the property of Romanticism as well as of Catholicism; and there is something of the Romantic infidel in both Villon and Barker. *The True Confession*'s literary ancestry includes Rousseau's *Confessions*, Baudelaire's proposed autobiography *My Heart Laid Bare*, Byron's *The Giaour*, De Quincy's confessions, and the atmosphere that pervades much literature from Goethe's *Werther* to Oscar Wilde's "The Ballad of Reading Gaol." In all but tone, it is very much like Saint Augustine's *Confessions*.

The early Christian saint's self-examination influenced Barker's novel *The Dead Seagull*, published in the same year (1950) as the first half of *The True Confession*. Book II of the poem makes the analogue clear; the introductory section ends with "Not much has happened to me save the Dies Irae/Dawning on Saint Augustine's City" (his *City of God*) and section four is informed by references to Augustine. The poet calls himself an "Augustinian anarchist," and further suggests the parallel, as well as a parallel to Eliot's *Waste Land* questor, with "To Hippo I came, yes, burning/With abominable passions/Seeking since I'm fond of learning,/The latest erotic fashions" (59).

Like Augustine, Barker traces his development through the

childhood search for assurance of a reality beyond the material world. Such a quest for belief is, of course, the theme of much modern literature and of two of the demigods of Barker's literary world—Eliot and Joyce. Like Augustine and Joyce, Barker writes spiritual autobiography. Augustine's search ends in Christian faith; Stephen Dedalus' in exile and triumphant esthetic isolation; Barker's in the contradictory position of the double man estranged from the faith he passionately desires. Although all three treat the isolating effects of sin, only Barker makes moral alienation and innocence painfully remembered opposites to be reconciled within the artistic structure. His poem is dialectical: although there is, especially in Book I, a sense of chronological development and the organization of a confession, there is no real resolution, no epiphanic moment of truth. The poet works off some of his rage, purges himself of obscenities by saying them, and, in his spiritual anguish, execrates both himself and God. In presenting the unresolved modern predicament, Barker is reminiscent of early Eliot. But the Byronic persona, unlike any of Eliot's masks of ineffectuality, achieves a kind of catharsis in hurling defiance at the same time that he resigns himself to his fate. Barker's voice is neither one of quiet desperation, nor one of wholly disaffiliated rage. The "questing beast" is on a religious tether.

In the Catholic Church confession is the act in which, after examining his conscience, a penitent accuses himself of his sins. In the first four sections of Book I, Barker explores, with considerable satiric wit, his sinful past; in the fifth section he makes his ironic confession:

> Good God, grant that, in reviewing
>   My past life, I may remember
> Everything I did worth doing
>   Seemed rather wicked in pursuing:
> Grant, Good God, I shall have remitted
>   Those early pleasures beyond number
> I necessarily omitted,
>   Exhausted by the ones committed (33).

The tone is irreverent, not to say blasphemous. God's mercies are recollected as blondes and brunettes. The double-edge cuts at God and at the speaker whose sorrow for his sins is implicit in the irony. He accuses himself, admits his moral responsibility, and recognizes God's suffering when he shut Him out in the act of illicit sex (35). Although in part the speaker ironically fulfills the requirements for penitence, he never expresses the firm purpose of amendment essential to true penance; he expects to transgress in the future. He asks God to let him recall his sins so that he can repent—"The places, faces and positions;/Together with the few additions/A feeble future may instill" (34).

And finally, although he ends Book I by asking for forgiving mercies, he does not have the firm faith that for Christ's sake the sins will be forgiven. He is wracked by doubt, unable to understand the paradox of man's supposed holiness and his suffering. Mockery counterpoints despair in Book II; written in Rome, it repeatedly questions God's inscrutable "mercies." Part 3 treats "The Grammar of Divine Assent:/I hear its silence everywhere . . ." The speaker derisively supplicates the Pope to intercede for man suffering the "Holy irony" (Part 5) of separation from God.

III   *The Leitmotifs of a Life*

Both Book I and Book II, like Villon's *Petit Testament*, begin by establishing the date and purpose for writing; Barker's general approach resembles, nevertheless, that of Villon's *Great Testament*. After recounting the wrongs of an impoverished childhood, he renounces love; but sour grapes derision is offset by a genuine sense of loss: "Deeper the love, greater the heart at breaking." Always searching, however, for the general principle in the specific event, Barker develops his denunciation into an indictment of the sex act itself, which he dissects as animal, biological, revolting, yet ambiguously glorious. He works toward a fury of ironic praise, finally undercut by his loathing:

> The act of human procreation,
>   —O crown and flower, O culmination
> Of perfect love throughout creation—
>   What can I compare to it?
> O eternal butterflies in the belly,
>   O trembling of the heavenly jelly,
> O miracle of birth! Really
> We are excreted, like shit. (Book I, 13)

What Barker's lines lack in good taste, they make up for in candor. The scatology forcefully expresses just how vulgar and disgusting the poet feels birth to be. Surely at this point the sentiment is almost Gnostic—almost a diabolical inversion of the value of life. Playing the antichrist, the speaker denies the act of life, in language reminiscent of Baudelaire who wrote of "a grudge or satire directed by Providence against love—and, thus, in the method of procreation, a sign of Original Sin. After all, we can make love only with the organs of excretion." [1]

Disgust with love is a recurring motif, revealed in each step of the poet's growth through the seven sections of Book I which correspond roughly to the seven ages of man. In Part 1, birth is degraded; in Part 2, the child is preoccupied with sex: he sees "phallic." In Part 3, the young seducer commemorates with a child the victims of his love. In Part 4, marriage is debased as mere sexual gratification—the joining of erogenous zones. Part 5 reveals a speaker obsessed with sexual guilt. For the father plagued by culpability for having "misled" children into life, the law of necessity is the paradox which leads him in Part 6 to implore and insist that the "harp and horror horned head" rest upon "That green regenerative breast/By whose great law we still live on." The jaded adult concludes, in Part 7, that life consists of a cycle of swilling, guzzling, and copulating "until/You break up like a jigsaw puzzle/Shattered with smiles" (41).

In Book II, less specifically grounded in autobiographical fact, love's failure is part of the total fabric; Section 5 is devoted to the divine irony of "the formula Love = MC^2" and the seventh to "Circe the Pythoness," the *femme fatale* love. The ninth part laments the injured Eros and records his death, while the eleventh reenforces archetypal suggestions of the bitch-goddess with references to the "Honeytongued bitch and Clytemnestra" and a "Dream of Fair Woman."

Developed in counterpoint to the motifs of alienation from God and disillusionment with love is the theme of loss of innocence. The speaker, tormented by memories of his romantic youth, asks, "Do Youth and Innocence prevail/Over that cloud cuckoo clime /Where the seasons never fail . . . ?" (18). He remembers early marriage as an innocent voyage in which ignorant explorers are blissfully unaware of the storms and hazards of the world (25).

But Eden ends in a vast "cemetary of innocence"; lost innocence derives from the original sin and fall of man:

> Look on your handwork, Adam, now
>   As I on mine, and do not weep.
> The detritus is us. But how
>   Could you and I ever hope to keep
> The glittering sibyl bright who first
>   Confided to us, perfect, once,
> The difference between the best and the worst?
>   That vision of our innocence. (41)

Another major theme of *The True Confession* is the poet's poetic development. A confession and a spiritual autobiography, it is also a literary history. Allusions to his own poetry make it another work about poetic growth. The ambivalent concept of Eros in *Eros in Dogma* is suggested when the speaker calls himself "Pig to the Circean Muse's honour"; the epithet suggests Barker's theory of the irresistible force of the creative imagination, of the adventure and enchantment of the creative act of transformation, of the spellbinding power of an art which the poet associates with eroticism. A reference to the Golden Calf alludes to the Golden Fleece elegy and the pain of "Moonstruck" love expressed there and in *The True Confession.* The atmosphere of early poems is evoked in the beginning of Part 11 of Book II with its *ubi sunt* motif: "They will not come again, the days/Auroral Anadyomene . . . That vision of the dawn . . ." And Barker reiterates and refers to the basic theme of his amorous verse, that love is predatory and the lover haunted by guilt, with

> You Villon murdered with a knife, but I
>   Like someone out of Oscar Wilde
> Commemorate with a child
>   The smiling victims as they die
> Slewing in kisses and the lie
>   Of generation. But we both killed. (21)

The "Bridal Nightmare" poems inform lines about his "Broken abandoned bride."

Repeatedly, Barker reminds the reader of the *Sacred and Secular Elegies.* Book I refers to the "Almighty God . . . whose ill

will" dominates the last "Sacred Elegy"; His remoteness from man
is the most tormenting problem of Book II. Living in Rome convinces the speaker more than ever of his moral isolation: "Are the
Gods with us? They are not"; as Antichrist, he asks "Now who by
who, my God, is mocked?" (Part 1). Because his despair is not
like that of the mystic undergoing the dark night of the soul, he
mocks himself: "Even though our star is crossed/It's not Saint
John in this Black Hole" (55). Hoping to dismiss his furies, he
asserts that we rationalize guilt and punishment—"invent/Out of
the heart afraid to die/The Avatars of the conscience,/The
Molochs of eternity" (61). He is awed at one moment with the
"intellectual/Inaccessibility" of the Logos (61) and at another
disgusted with man's anthropomorphism: "And there they squat,
the Three in One,/The Shapes of Man, the Apes of God" (77).
The final "Sacred Elegy" indeed parallels a major theme of *The
True Confession*.

IV   *A Style for Confession and Confrontation*

The True Confession is a dialectic of confession and confronta-
tion. Although charged with the emotions of the conflict, it is controlled technically by a form appropriate for objectifying thought
and emotion. Barker approximates Villon's ballade measure with
its eight octosyllabic lines and confines himself largely to the traditional rhyme scheme *ababbcbc;* the end rhymes are, however,
often half rhymes ("respects," "sex," "six," "pretexts"; "love,"
"dove," "give," "prove"), and the dominantly tetrameter lines are
not smooth and polished. The masculine brusqueness conveys the
speaker's impatience; the roughness, the dissonant tensions.

The poet relies on brash invocation and word play: "I invoke
him, dirty dog/As one barker to another" or "Come to me,
Grace, and I will take/You close into my wicked hand." Even the
puns indicate the mixture of the sacred and the profane; typically
Barker juxtaposes the innocent and the sardonic, the elevated
vocabulary of romance and religion—and reductive references to
the animal, the biological or the scientifically deterministic. Allusions to Classical mythology are contrasted to Christian references. The lines move rapidly from the sublime to the ridiculous,
emulating Byron and, at the same time, Auden in sometimes saving the most devastating undercutting for the final couplet of a
stanza. But, in tension with the slapdash cynicism of Book I, are

expressions of the feeling that is usually masked and controlled by
irony; Part 3 of Book I includes, for example, the bittersweet
lyric, "I sent a letter to my love."

Typically, however, Barker undercuts the pretentiously lofty
with the trite, the idealistic with the cynical, the supernatural with
the natural:

> And thus, incepted in congenial
>   Feebleness of moral power
> I became a poet. Venial
>   As a human misdemeanour
> Still, it gave me, prisoner
>   In my lack of character,
> Pig to the Circean Muse's honour.
> Her honour? Why, it's lying on her. (17)

Typical are the word-play (with its portmanteau effect) on "con-
genial" which the reader expects to be "congenital," the fearless
use of words dealing with moral categories and abstractions like
character, and the ambiguity of the last line whose pun on honor
produces a triple meaning—the plain sense (if, indeed, the reader
is willing to elide the period and assume that the first honor given
the poet was poetic esteem), the erotic implication, and the indi-
cation of the dishonest "on her" of his muse and his involvement
with her. The dominant tone is strongly reminiscent of Auden.

Significantly, Barker's satire is usually directed at himself.
Auden uses a more typically modern strategy in *The Age of Anxiety* where he does not identify with his characters. In poems by
Eliot and Auden irony is supposedly impersonal, but Barker
clearly turns criticism inward—sees his own pretensions and de-
flates them. In recognizing them, he is insisting upon his own
insignificance and moderating the egotism of his seemingly self-
centered poem. His approach is personal, not attenuated and in-
tellectualized. He gives us irony in its least complicated, but most
biting form.

The irony of self-appraisal is appropriate in a poem which turns
upon a private life and a personal attempt to make sense of an
admittedly irrational world:

> Since the Age of Reason's seven
>   And most of one's friends over eight,

> Therefore they're reasonable? Even
>   Sensible Stearns or simpleton Stephen
> Wouldn't claim that. I contemplate
> A world which, at crucial instants,
> Surrenders to adulterant infants
>   The adult onus to think straight. (16)

While asserting that, in a crisis, man reverts to the irrational, Barker (like Auden and MacNeice who also wrote a *Testament* based on Villon) lightly lampoons his literary compatriots—Eliot and Spender. Metaphysical speculation leads only to an impasse. The instinctive, amoral snake striking or the physicist applying reason to matter serve "better than those who advance a/Question to which life's the answer" (35). Like the religious Existentialist who believes that essence is created through existence, Barker recognizes the absurdity of modern life and belief, the importance of individual response and responsibility and the significance of irrational faith.

His persona is in many respects Kierkegaardian—despairing because of the claims of things temporal on him, suffering over guilt, but needing beyond all need to believe in the unbelievable. Tortured by the denials in his sense experience of any religious truth and, at the same time, intuiting such truth through need and guilt, he, like Kierkegaard, examines the one reality he is sure of—his own subjective existence. Such a quest is a search for self-identity and hence assurance of one's existence itself, an existence that is at bottom essentially ethical and religious. Barker's use of anti-climax reflects his recognition of the absurd and of his fear of self-estrangement, of the alienation of rational thought from religious sensibility and of action from belief. But, when the mockery leaves his voice, he confronts existence with passionate hostility or tragic resignation.

Book I ends in a bold, paradoxically sacrilegious plea for mercy—the mercy of death: "for our state/—Insufferable among mysteries—/Makes the worms weep. Abate, abate/Your justice. Execute us with mercies" (43). Like other anguished passages, it abandons anti-climax, this time to make the prayer for mercy simultaneously an expression of the thing that God finds unforgivable, the suicidal death-wish. In the very act of supplication, the Romantic completes his alienation.

Only in the last section of Book II is the Dionysian yea-sayer fully revealed. Here again addressing the "Master of the Thorny Ways," the poet moves toward tragic resignation, accepting as an analogy to men's lives the beauty and mystery of nature and of dawn that spellbound lovers cannot wake to. Instead of demanding rags to "suffocate/The orphan in its flaming cradle" (and hence demanding the end of the Christian era and of the unsponsored Christian life), as in the last section of Book I, the older poet implores that man be granted some vision of God's goodness and his promise of eternity—that man may, in terms befitting St. Paul, Augustine, and Kierkegaard, grasp eternity in one epiphanic moment: that he may

> Look up to see, like Aldebaran,
> The gold sunsetting mask of God
> Christening us with our day's
> Apotheosizing blaze
> Like Death hanging fire overhead.

Since he knows faith to be irrational, the modern man ends his spiritual autobiography asking for a sign, for some visible symbol of God. Luckily, the poet has already seen this presage of God in "the fanfares of the day" and in "Birds as of Paradise" who make us "know that the Eternal Tense/Crowns the Cloud of our Ignorance. . . ."

The dignity of the last section helps *The True Confession* to subsume and transcend the seemingly offensive language and ribald wordplay, the self-pity, the self-disgust, and the blasphemy of other sections and helps to make the kind of significant poetic statement that Barker had a right to want to include in his *Collected Poems.*[2] The danger of the poem is its tendency to lapse into pure statement, to become self-consciously clever, or to become, especially in Book II, an unrelieved compendium of mythological and Christian allusions or a series of queries, quips and critiques on religion, love, and even money, for "Money needs love and love needs money" (83). The lapses are short and sometimes entertaining, if one can forgive Barker his rambling structure. But the poem succeeds in spite of itself: it communicates the emotional, intellectual, and spiritual predicament of a twentieth-century Romantic, bitterly laughing in the dark.

CHAPTER 8

The English Bard and the Scotching Reviewers

BARKER'S reputation as a lyric poet is assured, but his poetry has never been fashionable. It has received only the sporadic attention of reviewers; of writers generalizing on the contemporary scene; and, more rarely, of critics appoaching his work from a limited point of view. David Daiches and Francis Scarfe wrote essays on his early lyricism;[1] Audrey Beecham and Vernon Scannell independently traced his development;[2] and Anthony Cronin declared that his ideas had been neglected.[3] Practically no extensive or intensive explication of his poetry is to be found outside of this book. C. Day Lewis' treatment of a sonnet in *The Poetic Image* is a notable exception which, finding much to admire, nevertheless objects to seemingly irrational imagery and to what he calls "impure poetry" of direct statement.[4]

Like Lewis, other critics both damn and praise Barker's style, acclaiming its "brilliance, its weight, its excitement," [5] and attacking its "heresies . . . such as frequent abuse of hyperbole and pathetic fallacy." [6] Geoffrey Grigson accused Barker of "muddled obscurity." [7] But, despite his vituperative review of the early poems, Grigson continued to advertise and to publish Barker's work in *New Verse*. Grigson, who admittedly prefers a more objective poetry, makes the mistake of most of Barker's detractors: they throw away the wheat with the chaff.

T. S. Eliot early recognized his merit, however,[8] and W. B. Yeats was so impressed with the early verse that he included several poems in *The Oxford Book of Modern Verse* (1892–1935). Clearly Yeats cared more about the personal note in "The Wraith-Friend" and in 'The Crystal" than about the "false words" and "elongated latinate forms" that Grigson condemned. Oscar Williams was so convinced of his genius that, as late as 1963, he devoted forty pages of his *Mentor Book of Major British Poets* to Barker. Critics on the side of detached reporting and rational discipline persisted, however, in their disapproval. Despite his own affinities to Romanticism, Stephen Spender discarded his one-time friend as "another poet of unreason who is intoxicated with words . . . essentially a naïf and clumsy writer uncertain of his meanings, hypnotised often with words and ideas which he understands imperfectly, but with a certain visionary power which often compels attention." [9]

The early and middle poems were usually noted for their lyricism and verbal intoxication; but whether "intoxication" is a positive or pejorative term depends upon the attitude of the user. In a decade dominated by the Pylon poets, Barker's originality inspired Francis Scarfe and David Daiches to commend his artistic nonconformity, while entertaining some reservations about and some hopes for his style. Scarfe welcomed a "pure" poet for his successful treatment of narcissism, nihilism, and permanent values, such as romantic love, which the social poets tended to overlook.[10] In his essay in *Poetry* Daiches lauded the personal note in Barker's identification with the parts of a crumbling society in a decade devoted to objective social criticism. Despite the dangers he thought inherent in Barker's method, he saw in his lyricism a new hope for poetry. In a review Daiches commended *Sacred and Secular Elegies* (1943) as "constructed with a kind of brilliant abandon . . . an ardor, a spontaneity, a passion (to use an unfashionable word). . . ." [11]

Babette Deutsch was even more accurate when, in surveying the techniques of Barker and Dylan Thomas, she wrote, "Their attack upon language is like a battering ram set against the mystery of the universe. . . ." [12] Lawrence Durrell, more appreciative and just than most, wrote

Barker is occupied with the task of bringing shape and order to a temperament which is essentially romantic, and a feeling for words which is sensual and musical. He is a master of vowel-sounds, and his poetry is . . . delicately and richly coloured. . . . His strong suit is not statement, but music and invocation. . . . Taming his romantic sensibility . . . often leads him to commit excesses in his verse—too facile invocation is one of his sins, and a tendency towards euphemism another.[13]

Durrell's response to Barker's grand style is typical.

Associated with verbal experiment and nonconformity, Barker's early and middle work (1933–1937; 1938–1949) was subject to much facile criticism. Subsequently, Barker chastened his style and even repudiated some of his best early "decadent" work; but commentators continued to object. Geoffrey Moore wrote that his use of Freudian symbols was designed to shock the bourgeois.[14] Although aware of some of Barker's merits, Vernon Scannell attacked his misuse of pathetic fallacy and his occasional failure to achieve sufficient detachment from the poems to see their faults.[15] Barker had, however, an answer for such criticism: his 1953 Shakespeare lecture insisted that in seeking the truth of human experience the poet must be granted a few "obscurities and pomposities." He admitted that he had "never been on the side of the angelic perfectionists . . . that perfect poetry is no more possible than perfect people," that "gigantic experiments" justify "gigantic mistakes."[16] Elsewhere he wrote: "In poems which have truly traversed and emerged from the imaginative machinery of a natural poet, all sorts of crude and undigested elements can be present without serious hurt or damage to the poem."[17]

Since most academic critics are "angelic perfectionists," it is not surprising that Barker's demonic passions, infernal imagery, and irreverent word play have not inspired extensive criticism. Writers for whom linguistic analysis is paramount overlook Barker's ideas. In 1953, however, Anthony Cronin had sufficient courage and perspicuity to assert in his essay, "Poetry and Ideas: George Barker," that concern for language diverts attention from the salient feature of Barker's work. In 1941, Harvey Breit had anticipated Cronin in recognizing astutely that Barker's view of the world is essentially moral and tragic.[18] Cronin extended the definition to call Barker a religious poet whose subject is "choice and the consequences of choice."[19] Religious feeling is at the heart of Barker's Romanticism. The man tormented by feral darkness contends for the sun. Influenced by a realism that his senses confirm, by the claims of biological and psychological determinism, and by evidences of man's inhumanity, he fights to affirm God and the Good. But his inner dualism creates dilemmas and denouements. A prototype of the modern Romantic, he struggles to integrate thought and sensibility.

A dialectic of verse which reconciles opposites is the appropriate correlative for this matrix of meaning. Because the antitheses and tensions mirror a vital dialectical process, it is a mistake to characterize style apart from meaning and feeling in Barker's poems, just as it is wrong to assert that dissonant imagery is bad imagery when indeed it can reflect intense experience, or that statement per se is bad in poetry, when imagery may have earned the poet the right to statement. Apparently unwilling to let Barker's poems establish their own standards, critics have applied theirs to his verse. If they are embarrassed by unabashed subjectivity or think censoriously that certain symbols or subjects are unpoetic, they are likely to attack Barker as a sexual or moral exhibitionist. If readers look for logical structure and deny the omnipotent "I" imaginative vision, if they forget that poetry is the operation of the mind (not simply the *rational* faculty) on objects, if they ban irrational juxtapositions or eccentric, paradoxical imagery, if direct statement is their *bête noire*, if they prefer decorous, impersonal poetry and cannot affirm that there is poetry in passion, Barker will sometimes offend them.

Despite the usefulness of noting that Barker's work is written in two modes, one subjective and the other objective, Geoffrey Moore's emphasis on "competing" styles simply misses the point.[20] There is no real dichotomy: there are only poems, some highly personal and internalized and others recording responses to actual events. Barker handles a poem grounded in physical fact differently from one centered in psychological reality. Despite an undeniable unevenness in Barker's work, Moore mistakenly asserts that there is "a softness at the center. . . ." The core is rather a knot of tragic tensions which expresses major conflicts of our age. Barker lapses "into an embarrassing jumble of Freudian imagery"[21] only to the critic who refuses to accept associative organization of poetic materials or who is himself disturbed by poetic candor. The impact of the poem's frankness—or of Barker's emotional intensity mirrored in rich imagery—produces in a sympathetic reader the shock of recognition.

Modern fiction has long since won its battle for naturalistic detail; in its middle age, New Criticism need not demand of poetry, decorum or veiled treatment of sex. Readers influenced by New Critical thought sometimes consider poetry a craft whose rules and shibboleths can be learned; they forget the basic assumption that the poem is an organism to be judged by the criteria of its context. Barker's best poetry has organic unity. The experiences themselves are often intense and private; form reflects, reinforces,

and imparts meaning and feeling. The medium, as Marshall Mc-
Luhan would say, is the message. The charge of obscurity is irrelevant to the serious reader who does not expect a poem to disclose its mysteries at first reading. The best poems provide the
pleasures of esthetic recognition. They yield up, too, more than
the sense of vicarious experience, more than the challenge to em-
pathize with experience alien to our own. Barker's best work, like
all great poetry, engages and repays us, as anything of value does,
with repeated contact; and yet the initial reading often dazzles us
with its music and dramatic vitality. If we prefer delicacy and
detachment, we may not give a Barker poem the attention it re-
quires. We may dismiss Barker as a poseur, overlook his seriousness, and consequently miss the rewards of his verse.

To appreciate the poems we should perhaps differentiate, as
Thomas De Quincy did, between literature of power and literature of knowledge, thus reminding ourselves not to stress intellectual at the expense of emotional apprehension or to rely on analysis at the expense of synthesis. E. M. Forster's fable "The Celestial
Omnibus" warns of the dangers of learning without intuition, of
pride of intellect without humility in esthetic experience, of using
literature to enhance self-esteem without discovering that its primary function is to move us. Since few critics today genuinely
suspend disbelief before a poem, they do not take De Quincy's
distinction or Forster's admonition seriously; hence they are prepared to distrust Barker's passion and power. When he is most
successful, we are first stirred by his response to events in the
moral history of man. A true Romantic, he is rarely concerned
with ideas apart from feeling. Reading him can be an exercise in
tolerance, a study of romantic and religious reaction to an age of
secularism and reason, an education of the sensibility, and an exciting esthetic experience.

In 1959 Stephen Spender likened the modern critic to a giant
who throws a great rock at a little fly: he either smashes or misses
his prey.[22] Because so many writers have crushed, missed, or only
clipped Barker's wings—or, worse, have tried to scotch him with
pebbles—Barker remains a controversial figure. Unlike many of
his contemporaries, he hasn't gained the poetic notoriety that critical attention can create in an age of criticism. Any reader who is
not intimidated by giants, or taken in by literary biases, will find a
poetry remarkable for its power. If he does not reject Barker's

moral intensity, he will find poems, moving and musical, ranging from impassioned lyricism to symphonic grandeur to colloquial directness. A significant number combine compulsive rhetoric and fundamental brainwork to convey with courage and audacity Barker's *Sturm und Drang* Romanticism. At their best, they are a tonic for apathy and dilettantism, pedestrian rationalism and cool disaffiliation—a tonic for the times.

In *The Enchaféd Flood* W. H. Auden dismisses Romantic artists as outmoded in the modern age:

We live in a new age in which the artist neither can have such a unique heroic importance nor believes in the Art-God enough to desire it, an age, for instance, when the necessity of dogma is once more recognised, not as the contradiction of reason and feeling but as their ground and foundation, in which the heroic image is not the nomad wanderer through the desert or over the ocean, but the less exciting figure of the builder, who renews the ruined walls of the city. Our temptations are not theirs. We are less likely to be tempted by solitude into Promethean pride. . . . Let us, reading the logs of their fatal but heroic voyages, remember their courage.[23]

By Auden's definition, Barker is an anachronism; and solitary heroism is to be remembered but not honored today. Of course, Auden is wrong; Barker is not simply an eccentric alien in the twentieth century. His sense of guilt and estrangement, his struggle with morality and belief, his search for self-discovery, and his tragic affirmation are truly apposite in our troubled age.

His poetry—a paradigm of Wordsworth's "spontaneous overflow of powerful feelings" recollected in tranquillity[24]—communicates on the fundamental level of emotion. But he is never content with emotion for its own sake. Fierce moral vision compels him to write in judgment of the voice and the epoch in the poems. As seer and pariah, Barker despises callow cant and distrusts urbane reason. He cannot submerge spiritual problems in respect for man as a merely social being, nor can he conveniently separate moral from private or political behavior. He writes poetry of conscience. And, as the conscience of his times, he explores the effects of the people, the events, and the ideas of an era and a life upon the human heart. Tempering spontaneous emotion with organic form, balancing over the abyss of sentimentality or self-pity with the ballast of brilliant imagery, allusion, wit or self-irony, he takes us on a Romantic voyage. Believing in the importance of the poet's Promethean[25] task, he directs his muse to the quest for personal values. His poetry illustrates that Romantic tradition can be both respected and remade. He is indeed an archetype of Romanticism as it persists in the twentieth century.

Notes and References

Chapter One

1. "A Note on André Gide," *Life and Letters Today,* LX (February, 1949), 117–19.
2. *The London Magazine,* III (September, 1956), 49–54.
3. *Ibid.,* p. 54.
4. Cf. "Verses for the 60th Birthday of Thomas Stearns Eliot," *News of the World* (London, 1950), p. 37.
5. Cf. "Funeral Eulogy for Garcia Lorca," *Life and Letters Today,* XXIII (October, 1939), 63.
6. *Ibid.*
7. Cf. Dedication to *Calamiterror,* dated 1936. Barker calls his brother "my Hell hand's Abel."
8. During his early days in London, Barker "informally seceded from the Roman Catholic Faith" ("Coming to London," p. 53); the speaker in *Janus* asserts himself to be "Free of the attritional ethics affixed to me in childhood" (49); in *Alanna Autumnal* the young man muses, "I respect neither my country nor myself nor any ethical regulations I have ever investigated" (25). But when the author visited Barker in London in the summer of 1963, he alleged that his remarks were "a joke." He is, as he wrote of James Joyce, on a religious tether. Cf. "James Joyce, Heretic," *Nation,* CLV (February 21, 1942), 236–37 (Review of *James Joyce* by Harry Levin).
9. "A Note on the Dialectics of Poetry," *Purpose,* XI (January–March, 1938), 27–30.
10. "Therefore All Poems are Elegies," Foreword to *New Poems: 1940,* ed. Oscar Williams (New York, 1941), pp. 15–18.
11. "Poet as Pariah," *New Statesman and Nation,* XL (July 8, 1950), 37–38; "William Shakespeare and the Horse with Wings," *Partisan Review,* XX (July, 1953), 410–20; "The Face Behind the Poem," *Encounter,* VI (May, 1956), 69–72.
12. "William Shakespeare," p. 413.
13. *Ibid.,* p. 417.
14. "A Study of Robert Bridges," *Nation,* CLIV (April 4, 1942), 400.

15. "Note on Dialectics," p. 30.

16. "William Shakespeare," pp. 410–11.

17. "Note on André Gide," p. 117.

18. "Note on Dialectics," p. 30.

19. *Ibid.*, p. 29.

20. *Ibid.* Cf. also "The Chameleon Poet," review of E. M. Butler's *Rainer Maria Rilke, New Republic,* CV (October 27, 1941), 548.

21. "William Shakespeare," p. 411. Cf. also "Funeral Eulogy for Garcia Lorca," *Life and Letters Today,* XXIII (October, 1939), 63.

22. Review of Vernon Watkins' The Death Bell, *London Magazine,* I (August, 1954), 90.

23. "William Shakespeare," p. 420.

24. "The Chameleon Poet," p. 548.

25. "William Shakespeare," p. 416 & 415.

26. "Poet as Pariah," p. 37.

27. *Ibid.*, p. 27.

28. *Ibid.*, p. 28.

29. *Ibid.*, p. 29.

30. "William Shakespeare," p. 415.

31. *Ibid.*, p. 420. Cf. also "The Opinion of George Barker on Some Modern Verse," *Life and Letters Today,* LXIV (February, 1950), 133.

32. "Note on Dialectics," p. 29. In "William Shakespeare" Barker writes "The god Dionysus exacts his tributes. . . . This is the law of excess; it is absolutely essential for the poet to bite off more than he can chew" (p. 420). Nietzsche's Zarathustra propounds the dualism of light and darkness just as Barker does; Barker's "The Death of Manolete" (*Vision of Beasts and Gods,* 1954) can be interpreted as the myth of Dionysian darkness defeating Apollonian light, which changes the standard of values. In "At the Wake of Dylan Thomas" (*VBG*), Barker eulogizes Thomas as a Dionysian.

33. Francis Scarfe, *Auden and After* (London, 1942), p. 155.

34. "Apocalypse," *A New Romantic Anthology,* eds., H. Treece and S. Schimansky (London, 1949), p. 48.

35. Frederick Hoffman, "From Surrealism to the Apocalypse," *English Literary History,* XV (June, 1948), p. 17.

36. "The Personalist View of Romanticism," *A New Romantic Anthology,* p. 17.

37. *Ibid.*, p. 19.

38. Henry Treece, *How I See Apocalypse* (London, 1946), pp. 80–81, 74.

39. Hoffman, p. 154.

40. Walford Morgan, "Notes on Contemporary Tendencies," *A New Romantic Anthology,* p. 55.

41. G. S. Fraser, Quoted in *How I See Apolcalypse,* p. 75.

42. Wallace Fowlie, *Age of Surrealism* (New York, 1950), p. 177.
43. Scarfe, p. 146.
44. "Note on Dialectics," p. 28.
45. Herbert Read, *Surrealism* (London, 1936), p. 40.
46. Quoted in Henry Treece, *Dylan Thomas* (London, 1949), ft. nt. 1, p. 47.
47. Hoxie N. Fairchild, *The Romantic Quest* (Philadelphia, 1931), p. 251.
48. "William Shakespeare," p. 415.
49. Jacques Barzun, *Romanticism and the Modern Ego* (Boston, 1947), p. 70.

Chapter Two

1. Answers to an Enquiry, *New Verse*, XI (October, 1934), 22.
2. Middleton Murry, *William Blake* (London, 1933). Cf. "The Revolt of Orc," p. 85. The sons of joy seek the "state of perfection . . . a condition of free development of Identity, through the continual annihilation of the Self [the egocentric, rational self] in all its forms." p. 33.
3. *Ibid.*, p. 88.
4. Cf. Blake's *Milton*, plate #47. British Museum copy.
5. Some of the early poems, like "He Comes Among," evoke a vague Ideal of Beauty through suggestive, blurred impressions and try to convey transcendent experience through symbols in the manner of the Symbolists. Furthermore, the Symbolist idea that poetry should aspire to the condition of music finds its way into much of the poetry, but Barker is not an esthete and his music is rarely pure.

Chapter Three

1. "William Shakespeare," p. 411.
2. C. G. Jung, *Psychology of the Unconscious* (New York, 1947), p. 92.
3. Elizabeth Drew, T. S. Eliot, *The Design of His Poetry* (New York, 1953), p. 414.
4. Jung, p. 207.
5. Jung, *Aion* (New York, 1959), p. 37.
6. Drew, pp. 142–43.
7. Jung, *Psychology,* p. 160.
8. *Ibid.*, p. 171.
9. Barker, who is closely identified with his persona, moved to a Dorset cottage in 1935.
10. Blaise Pascal, *Pensées* (London, 1931), #72.
11. William Wordsworth, *Intimations Ode*, V, ll. 68–77.
12. *Ibid., The Prelude*, VIII, ll. 478–79.

13. *Ibid.*, ll. 677–78.
14. *Ibid., The Recluse*, ll. 788–94.

Chapter Four

1. "Therefore All Poems are Elegies," p. 18.
2. "Reviews," *The Adelphi*, IV (June, 1932), 641.
3. Stephen Spender, *World Within World* (New York, 1948), p. 175.
4. *Elegy on Spain* (Manchester, 1939).
5. *New Verse* enquiry.
6. Mario Praz tabulates the evidence for the ecstatic agonies of Romantic love in his somewhat specialized study of Romanticism, *The Romantic Agony* (New York, 1956).
7. "The Death of Yeats," *Selected Poems* (New York, 1941), p. 40.
8. E. F. F. Hill, *A New Romantic Anthology*, p. 39.

Chapter Five

1. *Cain*, II, l. 2.
2. *New Yorker*, XVIII (July 25, 1942), 16, 18.
3. *New Republic*, CV (December 8, 1941), 792.
4. *Ibid.*, p. 794.
5. Malcolm Cowley, "Three Poets," *New Republic*, CV (November 10, 1941), 625.
6. *Pensées*, p. 84.
7. E. M. Butler, *Rainer Maria Rilke* (Cambridge, 1941), pp. 326, 327.
8. "The Chameleon Poet," p. 548.
9. Butler, pp. 330, 329.
10. "Rilke," *New Statesman and Nation*, XVIII (August 19, 1939), 276.
11. Jung, *Aion*, p. 112.
12. In *The Dead Seagull*, when Marsden's lover tries to leave her, they quarrel. She behaves "like a feline, on her haunches. Without another sound she springs, her eyes dazzling with hatred and the passion to kill, straight at my face. I struck at her as I would have struck a female panther" (85). The narrator explains his love for her and her symbolic significance: "I love her because she is an animal as incapable of sin as a tigress. She has no soul. I see in her not the misery of man separated from his creator but the defiance of the beast who cannot envisage god" (103). Marsden too has a head that destiny never worried and, like Nature, controls destinies with her irresistible attractions.
13. The lover in *The Dead Seagull* says, "You might be persuaded to think the truth quite simple, that I want to possess both Theresa and Marsden. If only it were as simple as that! No, Providence is my

black beast. How dare she create them separate, these two who are so incontestably one?" (89).

14. W. H. Auden, "Eros and Agape," *Nation*, CLII (June 28, 1941), 756.

15. Denis de Rougemont, *Love in the Western World* (New York, 1957), p. 72.

16. Cf. Byron's note to *Childe Harold*, Canto II, l. 369.

17. Oscar Williams printed it in his *Little Treasury of Modern Verse* (New York, 1946) and later reprinted it in his *Mentor Book of Major British Poets* (New York, 1963).

Chapter Six

1. T. S. Eliot, *Selected Essays* (New York, 1950). Barker would have been particularly interested in Eliot's assertion that Baudelaire's life is "one which has grandeur and exhibits heroism" (p. 381).

2. Charles Baudelaire, "Journals and Notebooks," *The Essence of Laughter and Other Essays, Journals, and Letters* (New York, 1956), p. 210.

3. Although his critical works were not originally published under this title, it is a title Baudelaire devised and which his modern editors used. Cf. *The Mirror of Art* (Garden City, N. Y., 1956).

4. *The Essence of Laughter*, p. 179.

5. *Ibid.*, p. 169.

6. *Ibid.*, p. 186.

7. *Ibid.*, p. 177.

8. "Coming to London," p. 50.

9. Introduction, *Collected Poems of Michael Roberts* (London, 1958), p. 20.

10. *Ibid.*

11. This suggests Barker's acquaintance with the vocabulary of Kantian idealism, which Coleridge uses in the *Biographia Literaria*.

12. Conrad Bonifazi summarizes the generally accepted notion of Nietzsche's growing paranoic feelings of martyrdom in *A Comparison of Kierkegaard and Nietzsche* (London, 1953), pp. 79, 99.

13. Jung, *Psychology*, p. 404.

14. *Poetry*, LXXXVI (April, 1955), 8–9. Also in *London Magazine*, II (July, 1955), 26–28.

15. *Two Plays* (London, 1958).

Chapter Seven

1. *The Essence of Laughter*, pp. 183–84.

2. Faber and Faber, Barker's publisher, requested that *The True Confession* be omitted from the *Collected Poems*. Cf. page 13, *Collected Poems*.

Chapter Eight

1. David Daiches, "The Lyricism of George Barker," Poetry, LXIX (March, 1947), 336–46; Francis Scarfe, "George Barker, A Pure Poet," Auden and After (London, 1942), pp. 118–30.

2. Audrey Beecham, "George Barker," Life and Letters Today, XXV (April–June, 1940), 273–81; Vernon Scannell, "George Barker: Deep or Drumlie?" The Poetry Review, XLV (October–December, 1954), 223–25.

3. Anthony Cronin, "Poetry and Ideas: George Barker," London Magazine, III (September, 1956), 44–52.

4. Cecil Day Lewis' The Poetic Image (London, 1947), pp. 128–30. Oscar Williams' posthumous anthology, Masterpoems of the English Language (New York, 1966), contains an essay by the author of this book, explicating the "Three Memorial Sonnets," one of which Lewis treats.

5. Harvey Breit, "View of the World," Poetry, LIX (December, 1941), 159.

6. F. C. Golffing, "Mr. Barker and His Critics," Poetry, LXXII (April, 1948), 35.

7. "Nertz," New Verse, XV (June, 1935), 17. Grigson is an urban writer who continued to disapprove of Edith Sitwell, Dylan Thomas, and Barker. Cf. G. S. Fraser, The Modern Writer and His World (London, 1953), pp. 267, 337. Kenneth Rexroth's "Introduction" to New British Poets (New Directions, n.d.) refers to Barker's obscurity too; cf. xvi–xvii. A. S. Collins writes that "with the poets who succeeded them [the Auden group], Dylan Thomas, George Barker, David Gascoyne, poetry again became obscure." English Literature of the Twentieth Century (London, 1951), p. 107.

8. Cf. "Coming to London," p. 54.

9. Stephen Spender, Poetry Since 1939 (London, 1946), p. 7.

10. Scarfe, pp. 122–23.

11. Poetry, LXIV (April, 1944), 37.

12. Poetry in Our Time (New York, 1952), p. 347.

13. Key to Modern Poetry (London, 1952), p. 200.

14. "Wild Words and Personal Symbols" (review of Collected Poems), New York Times (November 16, 1958), p. 52.

15. Scannell, pp. 223–25.

16. "William Shakespeare and the Horse with Wings," p. 411: "It is to him [Shakespeare] that we owe the rigorous luxury of being able to put anything—anything at all—into a poem . . . all subjects in the hands of the poet proper, were poetic subjects." Cf. also, p. 415.

17. Review of Vernon Watkins' The Death Bell, London Magazine, I (August, 1954), 90.

18. Breit, p. 159.
19. Cronin, p. 44.
20. Moore, p. 52.
21. *Ibid.*
22. In a lecture at Washington and Lee University, Lexington, Va.
23. W. H. Auden, *The Enchaféd Flood* (New York, 1950), p. 153.
24. Cf. Preface to the second edition (1800) of the *Lyrical Ballads.*
25. Cf. "The Face Behind the Poem," p. 72.

Selected Bibliography

PRIMARY SOURCES

I. *Poetry Collections*
Thirty Preliminary Poems, London, The Parton Press, 1933.
Poems, London, Faber and Faber, 1935.
Calamiterror. London, Faber and Faber, 1937.
Elegy on Spain. Manchester, The Contemporary Bookshop, 1939.
Lament and Triumph. London, Faber and Faber, 1940.
Selected Poems. New York, The Macmillan Company, 1941.
Sacred and Secular Elegies. Norfolk, Connecticut, New Directions, 1943 (The Poets of the Year Series).
Eros in Dogma. London, Faber and Faber, 1944.
Love Poems. New York, The Dial Press, 1947.
News of the World. London, Faber and Faber, 1950.
The True Confession of George Barker. Denver, Colorado, Alan Swallow, (#2, Key Poets Series), 1950; London, Fore Publications, 1950; with Part II added, New York, New American Library, 1964.
A Vision of Beasts and Gods. London, Faber and Faber, 1954.
Collected Poems. London, Faber and Faber, 1957; New York, Criterion Books, 1958.
The View From a Blind I. London, Faber and Faber, 1962.

II. *Prose*
Alanna Autumnal. London, Wishart, 1933.
Janus. London, Faber and Faber, 1935.
The Dead Seagull. London, John Lehmann, 1950.

III. *Plays*
Two Plays ("The Seraphina" and "In the Shade of the Old Apple Tree). London, Faber and Faber, 1958.

IV. *Articles and Reviews*
Review of *New Signatures* and *New Bearings in English Poetry*, *Adelphi*, IV (June, 1932), 641–42.

Answers to an Enquiry, *New Verse*, XI (October, 1934), 22.
"16 Comments on Auden," *New Verse*, XXVI–XXVII (November, 1937), 23.
"A Note on the Dialectics of Poetry," *Purpose*, X (January–March, 1938), 27–30.
Review of *Shakespeare's Last Plays*, by E. M. W. Tillyard, *Purpose*, X (July–September, 1938), 182–84.
"Funeral Eulogy for Garcia Lorca," *Life and Letters Today*, XXIII (October, 1939), 61–65.
"All Poems are Elegies," Foreword, *New Poems: 1940* (Oscar Williams, ed.), New York: The Yardstick Press, 1941, pp. 15–18.
"When Greek Meets English," *Nation*, CLIII (August 23, 1941), 164–65 (Review of *Sophocles: Oedipus at Colonnus*, an English version by Robert Fitzgerald).
"Three Tenant Families," *Nation*, CLIII (September 27, 1941), 282 (Review of *Let Us Now Praise Famous Men*, by James Agee and Walker Evans).
"Huxley as Theologian," *Nation*, CLIII (October 11, 1941), 350 (Review of *Grey Eminence: A Study in Religion and Politics*, by Aldous Huxley).
"The Chameleon Poet," *New Republic*, CV (October 27, 1941), 548 (Review of *Rainer Maria Rilke*, by E. M. Butler).
"Saroyan Again," *Nation*, CLVII (November 9, 1941), 459 (Review of *The Beautiful People*, by William Saroyan).
"Notes from the Largest Imaginary Empire," *New Republic*, CV (December 8, 1941), 791–92.
"Poe as Symbol," *Nation*, CLIII (December 27, 1941), 673 (Review of *Edgar Allan Poe: A Critical Biography*, by Arthur Hobson Quinn).
"Henry Miller, Revivalist," *Nation*, CLIV (January 3, 1942), 17 (Review of *The Colossus of Maroussi*, by Henry Miller).
"Mr. Jolas," *Nation*, CLIV (February 7, 1942), 170 (Review of *Verticle*, ed. Eugene Jolas).
"James Joyce, Heretic," *Nation*, CLV (February 21, 1942), 236–37 (Review of *James Joyce*, by Harry Levin).
"In All Directions," *Nation*, CLIV (April 4, 1942), 347 (Review of *New Directions in Prose and Poetry, 1941*, ed. James Laughlin).
"A Study of Robert Bridges," *Nation*, CLIV (April 4, 1942), 400 (Review of *Robert Bridges: A Study of Traditionalism in Poetry*, by Albert Guerard).
"A Spray for the Nightingale," *New Republic*, CVI (April 13, 1942), 517–18 (Review of *Awake! And Other Wartime Poems*, by W. R. Rodgers).
"Improbable Empire," *The New Yorker*, XVIII: July 11, 1942, pp. 13–

16; July 25, 1942, pp. 16–18; August 8, 1942, pp. 16–17; September 19, 1942, pp. 19–21; October 31, 1942, pp. 22–23. Excerpt in *Scholastic*, XLII (April 19, 1943), 25–26.

"A Note on André Gide," *Life and Letters Today*, LX (February, 1949), 117–19.

"The Opinion of George Barker on Some Modern Verse," *Life and Letters Today*, LXIV (February, 1950), 131–33.

"Poet as Pariah," *New Statesman and Nation*, XL (July 8, 1950), 37–38.

"William Shakespeare and the Horse with Wings," (Text of a lecture delivered on Shakespeare's birthday at Stratford-on-Avon), *Partisan Review*, XX (July, 1953), 410–20.

"Dylan Thomas: Memories and Appreciations," *Encounter*, II (January, 1954), 16–17.

Review of Vernon Watkins' *The Death Bell* and Norman Nicolson's *The Pot Geranium*, *London Magazine*, I (August, 1954), 86–93.

"Coming to London," *London Magazine*, III (January, 1956), 49–54.

"The Face Behind the Poem (An Essay in Honor of Tennyson," *Encounter*, VI (May, 1956), 69–72. Reprinted in *Poetry*, XCVII (February, 1961), 310–15.

"The Poem in an Orange Wig," *Saturday Review*, XLIII (October 22, 1960), 15.

"Tennyson's Two Voices," *Master Poems of The English Language*, New York: Trident Press, 1966, pp. 654–57.

SECONDARY SOURCES

V. *Useful Studies, Comments, and Reviews of Barker's Poetry.*

BEECHAM, AUDREY. "George Barker," *Life and Letters Today*, XXV (April–June, 1940), 273–81. Traces Barker's development until 1940.

BREIT, HARVEY. "View of the World," *Poetry*, LIX (December, 1941), 159–62. Useful for emphasizing Barker's essentially moral and tragic world view.

CRONIN, ANTHONY. "Poetry and Ideas: George Barker," *London Magazine*, III (September, 1956), 44–52. A corrective essay which indicates, quite rightly, that emphasis on language has detracted from concern for Barker's ideas and his fundamentally religious preoccupation with "choice and the consequences of choice."

DAICHES, DAVID. "The Lyricism of George Barker," *Poetry*, LXIX (March, 1947), 336–46. A balanced appreciation lauding the personal note in Barker's lyricism, while entertaining some reservations regarding Barker's method.

DAY LEWIS, CECIL. *The Poetic Image*, London: Jonathan Cape, 1947, pp. 128–30. A critical explication of "The Seagull, Spreadeagled, Splayed on the Wind," one of Barker's "Three Memorial Sonnets."

FODASKI, MARTHA. "Three Memorial Sonnets," *Master Poems of the English Language* (ed. Oscar Williams), New York: Trident Press, 1966, pp. 1032–36. An introduction to the poet and detailed analyses of the three sonnets.

FRIAR, KIMON and John Malcolm Brinnin, "Myth and Metaphysics," *Modern Poetry* (an anthology), New York: Appleton-Century Crofts, 1951, pp. 436–40. Part of a stimulating essay on the metaphysical dilemma of the modern poet alienated from God is illustrated by Barker's last "Sacred Elegy."

GOLFFING, F. C. "Mr. Barker and his Critics" (Review of *Love Poems*), *Poetry*, LXXII (April, 1948), 34–38. Defends Barker's enthusiasm for "language *qua* language."

MOORE, GEOFFREY. "Wild Words and Personal Symbols" (Review of *Collected Poems*), *New York Times* (November 16, 1958), p. 52. Representative and all too cursory attack on Barker's "competing styles," Freudian imagery, and intellectual softness.

REXROTH, KENNETH. Ed. *The New British Poets*, Norfolk: New Directions, n.d., pp. xvi–xvii. Very brief, but suggestive introduction to Barker in a general survey of modern British poets.

SCANNELL, VERNON. "George Barker: Deep or Drumlie?" *The Poetry Review*, XLV (October–December, 1954), 223–25. Traces Barker's development and assesses him as an uneven poet.

SCARFE, FRANCIS. "George Barker: A Pure Poet," *Auden and After*, London: George Routledge & Sons Ltd., 1942, pp. 118–30. Appreciative study welcomes the early lyricism of a daring "pure" poet writing on subjects such as narcissism, nihilism and permanent values such as romantic love, which the social poets of the thirties tended to overlook.

SKELTON, ROBIN. "Allegory of the Adolescent and the Adult," *Master Poems of the English Language*, New York: Trident Press, 1966, pp. 1039–41. An explication of Barker's poem on adolescence, emphasizing Barker's use of sound effects to lend pattern to his poem.

Index